Victor W. Watton

Religion and Life
Revision Guide
THIRD EDITION

Although every effort has been made to ensure that website addresses are correct at time of going to press, Hodder Education cannot be held responsible for the content of any website mentioned in this book. It is sometimes possible to find a relocated web page by typing in the address of the home page for a website in the URL window of your browser.

Hachette UK's policy is to use papers that are natural, renewable and recyclable products and made from wood grown in sustainable forests. The logging and manufacturing processes are expected to conform to the environmental regulations of the country of origin.

Orders: please contact Bookpoint Ltd, 130 Milton Park, Abingdon, Oxon OX14 4SB. Telephone: (44) 01235 827720. Fax: (44) 01235 400454. Lines are open 9.00–5.00, Monday to Saturday, with a 24-hour message answering service. Visit our website at www.hoddereducation.co.uk

© Victor W. Watton 2003
First published in 2003 by
Hodder Education,
An Hachette UK Company
338 Euston Road
London NW1 3BH

Second Edition published in 2006.
This Third Edition published in 2010.

Impression number   5
Year   2014

Cover photos l–r: © Royal Observatory, Edinburgh/AATB/Science Photo Library; © Reuters/Corbis; © Digital Art/Corbis.
Typeset in 12/14pt Electra LH Regular by Gray Publishing, Tunbridge Wells.
Printed and bound in India.

A catalogue record for this title is available from the British Library.

ISBN: 978 0340 975 497

Contents

Introduction

This book is designed to support your revision of the Edexcel GCSE Religious Studies Specification: Unit 1 Religion and Life based on the study of Christianity and one other religion.

Each section of the book covers one of the four sections of the GCSE specification. Each section begins with a list of the key words you need to learn. Then each sub-topic within the specification for that section is covered as a separate topic. Each topic:

- has a summary of the key points
- outlines the main points needed to answer the explain questions (question c)
- gives arguments for and against the issues raised by the topic to make it easier to answer the response questions (question b) and the evaluation questions (question d).

Each section finishes with guidance on how to answer exam questions and an end of section test.

The book also contains an appendix to give you guidance on self-marking the end of section tests and how to improve your performance on the section tests.

How to use the book

You should revise all the topics in Section 1. In Sections 2, 3 and 4, for the topics which are about the attitudes of another religion other than Christianity, you should only revise *one religion* from Islam, Judaism, Hinduism or Sikhism.

1 Learn a section at a time.
2 Learn the key words of a section.
3 Work through each topic in a section in this way:
   - learn the key points
   - learn the main points
   - learn the advice on how to answer evaluation questions.
4 When you have learned all eleven topics, do the end of section test.
5 Use the mark scheme from Appendix 1 to mark your test, and go through the guidance on how to improve your performance. If you find it difficult to self-mark the test, visit www.hoddereducation.co.uk/religionandlife where there is a more specific mark scheme for each test.
6 Make sure you know everything about how to deal with the exam paper (see page 1 opposite) before you take the examination.

1. When you go into the exam hall and find your desk, your exam paper should be face up on the desk. Before you are allowed to open the paper, you can complete the front cover by:
   - writing your surname in the first top box
   - writing your first names in the adjoining box (if there is not enough room, write initials for those that will not fit)
   - writing your centre number (this will be on display in the hall) in the first box below
   - writing your personal exam number (you will receive this from your school before the exam) in the adjoining box.

   It is important that you get all of these completely correct, otherwise someone else may get your mark and grade!

2. When you are told to start, make a note of the time. You have 22 minutes per question (you could work on – part a) 2 minutes, part b) 4 minutes, part c) 10 minutes, part d) 6 minutes). You should try not to go beyond this as you will lose marks on Section 4 if you run out of time.

3. Start on Section 1 by choosing one of the questions, *either the whole of* question 1 (parts a, b, c, d) or *the whole of* question 2 (parts a, b, c, d). You should decide on which question to choose by whether you can do parts c) and d) as these are worth 14 marks of the 20 available.

4. Make sure you read the question carefully before you answer it and highlight key words such as *why, how, some, others, choose one religion other than Christianity*.

5. Make sure you put a line through the box beside the question you have chosen at the top of the first answer page. Your answers will be scanned and put onto a website, and the examiner will only be marking specific questions. If you do not indicate which question you have answered, your answer may not be marked.

6. If you run out of space, ask for a supplementary sheet of paper. The scanner does not pick up any writing outside the margins!

7. If you have any time left:
   - check that you have answered every part of each question
   - go through each answer to part c) checking the spelling and grammar and trying to add some extra specialist vocabulary, e.g. could you use any of the key words?
   - go through each part d) answer checking that you have three reasons for each point of view and adding reasons where necessary.

KEY WORDS FOR SECTION 1

Agnosticism	not being sure whether God exists
Atheism	believing that God does not exist
Conversion	when your life is changed by giving yourself to God
Free will	the idea that human beings are free to make their own choices
Miracle	something which seems to break a law of science and makes you think only God could have done it
Moral evil	actions done by humans which cause suffering
Natural evil	things which cause suffering but have nothing to do with humans
Numinous	the feeling of the presence of something greater than you
Omni-benevolent	the belief that God is all-good
Omnipotent	the belief that God is all-powerful
Omniscient	the belief that God knows everything that has happened and everything that is going to happen
Prayer	an attempt to contact God, usually through words

Topic 1.1 Religious upbringing

Main points

The main features of a Christian upbringing

Christian parents:

- are likely to have their babies baptised, when they promise to bring up their children to believe in God and be good Christians
- will teach their children to believe in God
- will teach their children to pray to God
- will take their children to worship God in church
- may send their children to a Church school.

How a religious upbringing may lead to, or support, belief in God

Children who have had a Christian religious upbringing may feel it is natural to believe in God because:

- Their parents will have told them about God and they will believe their parents.
- Christians pray to God, so they will believe that God exists because their parents would not waste their time praying to nothing.
- Seeing so many people worshipping God when they go to church will make them believe that God exists.
- They will be taught that God exists when they go to Sunday school, or Church school, and will believe it because their teachers tell them it is true.

> ## Key points
>
> Having a religious upbringing is likely to lead to belief in God because children who have a religious upbringing:
>
> - are taught that God exists
> - spend most of their time with people who believe that God exists.

Evaluation questions

You may be required to argue for and against having a religious upbringing.

1. People who think a religious upbringing is a good thing, may use these arguments:
   - A religious upbringing helps to keep a family together as parents and children join together for religious activities.
   - A religious upbringing gives children an understanding of what is right and wrong, and gives them good morals.
   - A religious upbringing gives children a sense of belonging and community, giving them emotional stability.

2. People who think a religious upbringing is a bad thing, may use these arguments:
   - A religious upbringing means children are brought up following a religion they have not chosen themselves.
   - Some people think that a religious upbringing can take away a child's human right to freedom of religion.
   - A religious upbringing can reinforce and continue religious prejudices which are harmful to society.

Topic 1.2 Religious experience

Key points

- Religious experience is when people feel God's presence.
- People claim to experience God in miracles, answered prayers, and the numinous.
- Religious experience makes people feel that God is real, and so they believe he must exist.

Main points

Religious believers who have had a religious experience will find that the experience makes their belief in God stronger because they believe they have had direct contact with God.

The **numinous** is a feeling of the presence of God. When people are in a religious building, in a beautiful place or looking up at the stars on a clear night, they may be filled with the awareness that there is something greater than them, which they feel to be God. Such a feeling is likely to lead you to believe in God.

Conversion is used to describe an experience of God, which is so great that people experiencing it want to change their life or religion and commit themselves to God in a special way. Conversion experiences make people believe in God because they feel that God is calling them to do something for him.

A **miracle** is an event that breaks a law of science and can only be explained by God. If you experience something that seems to break all the laws of science, you will look for an explanation, and if the only explanation you can think of is a miracle, you will start believing in God.

Religious believers think they can make contact with God through **prayer**. If the person praying feels that God is listening to the prayer, then they are likely to believe that God exists. Also, an answered prayer (for example, when someone prays for a sick loved one to recover and they do) will lead to belief in God.

Evaluation questions

You may be required to argue for and against religious experience proving God's existence.

1. People who think it does may use these arguments:
   - If you become aware of a presence greater than you in a numinous experience, you will believe that God must exist.
   - If you experience something that seems to break all the laws of science, and the only explanation you can think of is God, you will start believing in God.
   - If a person prays and their prayer is answered (for example, when someone prays for a sick loved one to recover and they do) they will believe God must exist.

2. People who think it does not may use these arguments:
   - A numinous experience is caused by your surroundings, whether a church or the stars, and may have nothing to do with God.
   - All miracles can be explained. For example, Jesus may not have been dead when he was taken down from the cross and so he just recovered rather than rising from the dead.
   - There are more unanswered prayers than answered ones, so they surely prove God does not exist.

Topic 1.3 The argument from design and belief in God

Main points

Design means making a plan to produce something. For example, a car is made to the plan of the designer, and looking at any part of the car makes you think that the car has been designed.

Many religious believers have looked at the world and seen that the way the universe works makes it look as if it has been designed. Some scientists also see evidence of design in the process of evolution where complex life-forms develop from simple ones. From this they have developed the argument from design:

- Anything that has been designed needs a designer.
- There is plenty of evidence that the world has been designed (laws of science such as gravity and magnetism; DNA being a blueprint for life, etc.).
- If the world has been designed, the world must have a designer.
- The only possible designer of the universe would be God.
- Therefore the appearance of design in the world proves that God exists.

This argument supports belief in God and may lead those who are not sure to believe there is a God.

Key points

- The universe seems to be designed.
- Anything that is designed must have a designer.
- God must therefore exist because only God could have designed the universe.

Evaluation questions

You may be required to argue for and against the design argument.

1. People who think the design argument proves God's existence may use these arguments:
   - There is plenty of evidence that the universe has been designed (for example, laws of science, DNA, evolution).
   - If something has been designed, it must have a designer.
   - Only God could design something as wonderful as the universe.
   - Therefore God must exist.

2. People who think the argument from design does not prove God exists may use these reasons:
   - No designer would have created things like volcanoes, earthquakes, etc.
   - Science can explain the appearance of design without needing God.
   - The argument does not explain how things like dinosaurs could have been part of a design plan for the world.
   - Even if the argument worked, it would only prove that the universe has a designer, not God.

Topic 1.4 The argument from causation and belief in God

Key points

- The way everything seems to have a cause makes people think the universe must have a cause.
- The only possible cause of the universe is God.
- So God must exist.

Main points

Causation is the process of one thing causing another. For example, a driver pressing the brake pedal causes the effect of the car slowing down.

The argument from causation is:

- Cause and effect seem to be a basic feature of the world. Whatever we do has an effect. If I do my homework (cause), I will please my parents and/or teachers (effect). Modern science has developed through looking at causes and effects, and scientific investigations seem to show that any effect has a cause and any cause has an effect.
- This means that the universe, the world and humans must have had a cause.
- God is the only logical cause of the universe.
- Therefore God must exist.

Evaluation questions

You may be required to argue for and against the argument from causation.

1. People who think the argument proves God's existence may use these reasons:
   - The argument makes sense of ourselves and the universe because it explains how and why we are here.
   - The argument fits in with our common sense. We cannot believe that something can come from nothing and the argument shows that everything came from God.
   - The argument fits in with science which tells us that every effect has a cause and so the universe (an effect) must have a cause (God).
   - We believe that things must have started off, they must have a beginning; and the argument explains that God started off the universe.

2. People who think the argument from causation does not prove God's existence may use these reasons.
   - If everything needs a cause then God must need a cause; why should the process stop with God?
   - It is possible that matter itself is eternal and so was never created. That would mean that the process of causes could go back for ever.
   - Just because everything in the universe needs an explanation does not mean the universe needs an explanation. The universe could just have been there for ever.
   - Even if there was a First Cause it would not have to be the God of any particular religion. It could be good, evil, a mixture of good and evil, several gods, etc.

Topic 1.5 Why scientific explanations of the world may lead to agnosticism or atheism

Main points

Science explains how the world came into being in this way:

- Matter is eternal.
- About 15 billion years ago, the matter of the universe exploded. This is known as the Big Bang theory. The red shift in light from other galaxies is evidence that the universe is still expanding.
- As the matter of the universe flew away from the explosion, it formed stars and then our solar system.
- The gases on the Earth's surface produced primitive life.
- The genetic structure of these primitive life-forms led to the evolution of new life-forms and, about 2.5 million years ago, humans evolved. (The evidence of fossils shows new life-forms coming into existence and genetic research shows the similarities of life-forms, for example 50 per cent of human DNA is the same as that of a cabbage.)

How the scientific explanation of the world may lead to agnosticism or atheism

If science can explain the universe and humans without God, it can lead some people to be agnostic, as they no longer need God to explain why we are here.

Other people may become atheists because they believe that if God existed, he must have made the world and be the only explanation for it. So the way that science can explain the world and humans without God is proof to such people that God does not exist.

Key points

Science says that matter is eternal and that the universe began when this matter exploded. The solar system came out of the explosion, and the nature of the Earth allowed life to develop through evolution.

Evaluation questions

Advice on answering evaluation questions is after Topic 1.6 on page 8.

Topic 1.6 How one religion responds to the scientific explanations of the world

Key points

- Many Christians accept the scientific explanations but believe they show that God created the universe through the Big Bang.
- Some Christians say the scientific explanations are wrong and the biblical story of creation is fact because it is the word of God.
- Some Christians believe that both science and the Bible are true because one of God's days could be billions of years.

Main points

There are three Christian responses to scientific explanations of the world.

Response one

Many Christians believe that the scientific explanations are true and prove that God created the universe because they believe:
- Only God could have made the Big Bang at exactly the right microsecond to form the universe.
- Only God could have made the laws such as gravity which the matter of the Big Bang needed to form solar systems.
- Only God could have made the gases on Earth react in such a way to form life.

Response two

Some Christians believe that all the evidence for the Big Bang and evolution can be explained by the Bible account of creation, Noah's flood and the Apparent Age theory. This claims that when Adam was made, the Earth was six days old, but to Adam it would have looked billions of years old because of the way God created it. So they believe science is wrong and the Bible is right. This response is known as creationism.

Response three

Some Christians believe that both the scientific explanations and the Bible are correct. They claim that the main points of the Bible story fit with science, but one of God's days could be millions or billions of years.

Evaluation questions

You may be required to argue for and against the scientific explanation of the world.

1. People who think the scientific explanation proves that God does not exist are likely to use such arguments as:
   - If God existed, he would be the only explanation of the world. Therefore the fact that science can explain the world and humans without God is proof that God does not exist.
   - The Big Bang was an accident and there is no evidence that it was caused by God.
   - An omnipotent and omniscient God would not have created the world in such a wasteful way.

2. You should use the Christian responses one and/or two above to argue against this.

Topic 1.7 Why unanswered prayers may lead to agnosticism or atheism

Main points

If people say their prayers in church and at home, but never feel the presence of God when they pray, they may feel there is no God listening to them. The feeling that no one is listening to their prayers leads them to **agnosticism**, or even **atheism**.

Unanswered prayers are even more likely to lead people to believe God does not exist. If someone's prayers are not answered, particularly if they are praying for something like a child to be cured of cancer or for the end of human suffering in wars, droughts, etc., then they might stop believing in God. This is because they may think God could not exist if he let such things happen. In this way, unanswered prayers can lead a person to become an agnostic or an atheist.

Key points

If people do not feel God's presence when they pray, or if people pray for good things, but their prayers are not answered, they may start to doubt God's existence. If God does not answer prayers, how do you know he exists?

Evaluation questions

Advice on answering evaluation questions is after Topic 1.8 on page 10.

Topic 1.8 How one religion responds to unanswered prayers

Key points

Christians believe that God cannot answer selfish prayers. But he answers all other prayers, although not always in the way people expect, because his answers have to fit in with his overall plans.

Main points

Most Christians believe that God answers all prayers and that what seems to be unanswered prayers can be explained by the following:

- Selfish prayers are answered, but not in the way the person praying may want. For example, if you prayed for God to help you to pass an exam without any work, God will answer the prayer by not helping so that you work hard next time.
- Your prayer may not be answered in the way you expect because God has different plans, for example he may want an ill person to enter heaven.
- Christians believe that God loves people and so they believe God's love will answer their prayers in the best possible way, even though it may not look like a direct answer.
- Christians have faith that God will answer all prayers in the best way for the person praying, or the people prayed for, even if it is different from what they expected.

Evaluation questions

You may be asked to argue for and against unanswered prayers proving that God does not exist.

1. People who believe that unanswered prayers prove God does not exist are likely to use such arguments as:
   - Christians believe that God is their loving heavenly Father who will answer their prayers, so if he does not answer them, he cannot exist.
   - Christians are told about answered prayers. For example, people being cured of terminal cancer by prayer, but far more people have their prayers unanswered. A good God would not answer a few prayers for a cure and not answer lots of prayers for a cure. Therefore it is unlikely that God exists.
   - If there was a God, he would answer the prayers of good religious people, and there would be no wars, no starvation, etc. The prayers of such people are clearly not answered, so God cannot exist.

2. People who think unanswered prayers do not disprove God's existence are likely to use such arguments as:
   - Your prayer may not be answered in the way you expect because God has different plans. For example, he may want an ill person to enter heaven.
   - Just like a human parent, God may answer our prayers by giving us what we need rather than what we have asked for.
   - Christians believe that God loves people and so they believe God's love will answer their prayers in the best possible way, even though it may not look like a direct answer.

Topic 1.9 Why evil and suffering may lead to agnosticism or atheism

Main points

Evil and suffering can take two forms:

- **Moral evil** is caused by humans using their free will. Wars and crimes such as rape, murder and burglary are good examples of moral evil.
- **Natural evil** is suffering that has not been caused by humans. Earthquakes, floods, volcanoes, cancers and so on are not caused by humans, but they result in lots of human suffering.

How evil and suffering cause people to question or reject belief in God

Philosophers express the problem in this way:

- If God is **omnipotent** (all-powerful), he must be able to remove evil and suffering from the world.
- If God is **omni-benevolent** (all-good), he must want to remove evil and suffering from the world.
- It follows that, if God exists, there should be no evil or suffering in the world.
- As there is evil and suffering in the world, either God is not all-good and powerful or he does not exist.

Also, if God knows everything (**omniscient**), he must have known the evil and suffering that would come from creating the universe. So he should have created the universe in a way that avoided evil and suffering.

Most religious believers believe that God is omnipotent, omni-benevolent and omniscient. So the existence of evil and suffering challenges their beliefs about God.

For many religious believers, evil and suffering become a problem if they experience it (for example, they are in an earthquake, or their child dies from a disease), when it can change them into an atheist or an agnostic.

Key points

Some people do not believe in God because they think that there would be no evil and suffering in a world created by a good and powerful God. A good God should not want such things to happen, and a powerful God ought to be able to get rid of them but does not.

Evaluation questions

Advice on answering evaluation questions is after Topic 1.10 on page 12.

Topic 1.10 How one religion responds to the problem of evil and suffering

Key points

Christians respond to the problem of evil and suffering by:

- praying for those who suffer
- helping those who suffer
- claiming that evil and suffering are the fault of humans misusing their free will
- claiming that evil and suffering are part of a test to prepare people for heaven.

Main points

Christians respond to the problem of evil and suffering in several ways. Most Christians would use at least two responses to explain how an all-good, all-powerful God can allow evil and suffering.

Response one

Many Christians believe from the Bible that God must have a reason for allowing evil and suffering, but humans cannot understand it, so the correct response of Christians is to follow the example of Jesus and fight against evil and suffering. Jesus fought evil and suffering by healing the sick, feeding the hungry, challenging those who were evil and even raising the dead. Christians do this by praying for those who suffer and by helping those who suffer. Many Christians become doctors, nurses and social workers, for example, so that they can help to reduce the amount of suffering in the world.

Response two

Many Christians claim that, by giving humans free will, God created a world in which evil and suffering will come about through humans misusing their free will. So evil and suffering is a problem caused by humans, not God.

Response three

Many Christians believe that the evil and suffering involved in this life are not a problem, because this life is a preparation for paradise. If people are to improve their souls they need to face evil and suffering in order to become good, kind and loving. God cannot remove evil and suffering if he is going to give people the chance to become good people. But, in the end, he will show his omni-benevolence and omnipotence by rewarding the good in heaven.

Response four

Some Christians claim that God has a reason for not using his power to remove evil and suffering, but humans cannot understand it. God is divine and there is no way humans can understand his thoughts.

Evaluation questions

You may be asked to argue for and against evil and suffering proving that God does not exist.

1. People who believe evil and suffering prove that God does not exist are likely to use such arguments as:
   - If God is omnipotent, he must be able to remove evil and suffering from the world. If God is omni-benevolent, he must want to remove evil and suffering from the world. It follows that, if God exists, there should be no evil or suffering in the world. As there is evil and suffering in the world, God does not exist.
   - A good God would not have designed a world with floods, earthquakes, volcanoes, cancers, etc. These cannot be blamed on humans and so they are evidence that God did not make the world and so does not exist.
   - An all-powerful God would not allow evil humans like Hitler and Stalin to cause so much suffering, so as individual humans have caused lots of suffering, God cannot exist.
   - God is supposed to be omniscient, so he would have known the evil and suffering that would come from creating this universe. Therefore, he should have created a different universe, and, as he did not, he cannot exist.

2. Christians believe evil and suffering do not disprove God's existence because:
   - The Bible shows that God must have a reason for allowing evil and suffering, but humans cannot understand it, so the correct response of Christians is to follow the example of Jesus and fight against evil and suffering.
   - By making humans with free will, God created a world in which evil and suffering will come about through humans misusing their free will. So evil and suffering is a problem caused by humans, not God.
   - The evil and suffering involved in this life are not a problem because this life is a preparation for paradise. If people are to improve their souls they need to face evil and suffering in order to become good, kind and loving. God cannot remove evil and suffering if he is going to give people the chance to become good people. But, in the end, he will show his omni-benevolence and omnipotence by rewarding the good in heaven.
   - God has a reason for not using his power to remove evil and suffering, but humans cannot understand it. God is divine and there is no way humans can understand his thoughts.

Topic 1.11 How two programmes about religion could affect a person's attitude to belief in God

Key points

You need to study two programmes about religion. For each one you will need to know:

- an outline of its contents
- how it might have encouraged some people to believe in God
- how it might have encouraged some people not to believe in God
- whether it affected your beliefs about God.

Main points

You have to study two programmes or films about religion in depth and work out how they could affect a person's attitude to belief in God.

From your class notes you should have:

- A summary of each programme.
- Four pieces of evidence from each programme to show how it might have encouraged some people to believe in God.
- Four pieces of evidence from each programme to show how it might have encouraged some people not to believe in God.
- What effect the programme had on your own attitude to belief in God and write down four reasons for this.

Evaluation questions

You may be asked to argue for and against programmes or films about religion affecting belief in God.

1. To show that programmes or films do affect beliefs about God, you should:
   Either
   - Use three pieces of evidence from a programme to show how it might have encouraged some people to believe in God.
   Or
   - Give three reasons why the programme affected your own attitude to belief in God.

2. To show how programmes or films do not affect beliefs about God, you should:
   Either
   - Use three pieces of evidence from a programme to show how it might have encouraged some people not to believe in God.
   Or
   - Give three reasons why the programme affected your own attitude to belief in God.

How to answer questions on Section 1

Up to four marks will be awarded for your spelling, punctuation and grammar in your answer to Section 1 of the exam paper. This means you should take extra care with your spelling and make sure you use full stops and capital letters. You should use paragraphs if your answers to parts c) and/or d) are long.
Four marks for spelling, punctuation and grammar can move an A to an A*, a B to an A, etc., remember to take extra care with your spelling and punctuation to answers in Section 1.

The a) question – key words

These questions give you up to two marks just for knowing the key words and their meanings. This means you must learn the key words because you can gain ten per cent of the marks if you get the a) questions right.

Have a look at the following examples.

Question

What is moral evil?   (2 marks)

Answer

Actions done by humans which cause suffering.

Two marks for a correct definition.

Question

What name is given to people who believe there is no God?   (2 marks)

Answer

Atheist.

Two marks for a correct definition.

The b) question – what do you think?

These questions give you up to four marks for giving your own opinion about one of the issues, but you will only gain marks if you give reasons for your opinion!

You must decide what you think about the issues and ideas you study. The questions are meant to be quite easy and to get full marks you just need to give two developed reasons. They are really like part i) of an evaluation question (question d)) where you have to give two reasons. So, to answer a response question, you could use two of the reasons from the point of view you agree with in the evaluation questions advice for each topic.

The following example shows you what is meant by developed reasons.

Question

Do you think miracles prove that God exists?
Give TWO reasons for your point of view. (4 marks)

Answer

I do not think miracles prove God exists because all miracles can be explained.

One mark for a reason.

For example, Jesus was not dead when he was taken down from the cross.

Two marks because the reason is developed.

Also miracles rely on the evidence of eye witnesses who could be lying ...

Three marks for a second reason.

... or they could be mistaken about what they saw.

Four marks because the second reason is developed.

Total = four marks.

The c) question – explain

You can gain two marks for giving a brief reason in basic English even if the spelling and grammar are poor. You will also only get two marks if you describe the issue rather than trying to explain it.

You can gain four marks by giving two brief reasons with a limited command of English and little use of specialist vocabulary.

You can gain five marks by giving three brief reasons, but this will rise to six marks if it is written in a clear style of English with some use of specialist vocabulary.

You can gain seven marks by using four brief reasons, but this will rise to eight marks if you write in a clear and correct style of English with a correct use of specialist vocabulary where appropriate.

Explain questions are where your Quality of Written Communication is tested, so you should answer these questions in a formal style of English, be careful with your spelling and try to use some specialist vocabulary. You can gain four extra marks on the paper if your written English is good, which could move an A to an A*, a B to an A, etc.

Have a look at the following example.

Question

Explain how a religious upbringing can lead to, or support, a belief in God.   (8 marks)

Answer

LEVEL 1: two marks for a reason expressed in basic English.

Christians usually teach their children to pray to God. This will make the children believe that God exists because otherwise their parents would not want them to pray to him.

LEVEL 2: by developing the reason, the answer goes up to level 2 and because the answer is written in clear English it would gain four marks.

If God did not exist, they and their parents would not waste their time praying to nothing. Also they may feel God's presence when they pray. So because they've been brought up to pray, they believe that God must exist.

LEVEL 3: by adding another reason the answer moves up to level 3 and because the answer is written in a clear style of English with some use of specialist vocabulary (pray, God's presence, church, worship) it would gain six marks.

Another feature of a Christian upbringing is going to church. When children go to church they see lots of people praying to God and worshipping God and this is bound to make them think that God must exist because all these people believe he does.

LEVEL 4: by adding a further reason, the answer moves up to level 4 and because it is written in a clear and correct style of English with extra specialist vocabulary (church school, RE lessons, exists) it would gain eight marks – full marks.

Many Christian parents also send their children to a church school. Here they will have RE lessons which teach them that God exists and the children are likely to believe it because their teachers tell them it is true.

The d) question – evaluation

To answer these questions you need to decide what you think about the quotation and then give three reasons for why you think that.

Then you need to give three reasons why some people (for example, Christians if you are an atheist, or atheists if you are a Christian) would disagree with you.

One of your points of view should always be religious so that you can give religious reasons.

Have a look at the following example.

Question

'Considering the evidence, everyone should be an agnostic.'

(i) Do you agree? Give reasons for your opinion.   (3 marks)
(ii) Give reasons why some people may disagree with you.   (3 marks)

Answer

(i) I do not agree because I am an atheist, not an agnostic.

> One mark for a personal opinion with a reason.

I think that science, the Big Bang, DNA and evolution are a compelling proof that God does not exist because he did not create the universe or people.

> The reason is developed so it moves up to two marks.

Also if God existed, surely he would have sent only one holy book, he would allow only one religion.

> The answer now gives another reason for the opinion, so it moves up to three marks.

Furthermore, the fact of evil and suffering in the world proves that God does not exist, because an all-good and all-powerful being would not allow it. The evidence of science, the problem of evil and suffering, and the huge problems of different religions convince me that there is no God and so I disagree with the statement.

> Although the last reason can gain no marks because the top level has already been reached, it is always worth writing an extra reason in case one is wrong.

(ii) I can see why some people would disagree with me because evidence such as design can be used both for and against God's existence.

> One mark for a reason why some people might disagree.

The design argument seems to prove God's existence, but the Big Bang seems to disprove it. In the same way the first cause argument seems to prove God's existence, but then there is the question of what caused God.

> The reason is developed so it moves up to two marks.

Then the religious evidence to prove God's existence such as miracles, holy books, etc. can be explained in non-religious ways. So it seems logical to say there is not enough evidence either way, so they are agnostics.

> The answer now gives another reason for some people disagreeing, so it moves up to three marks.

> This answer to question d) can gain full marks because both parts refer to religious reasons and the question did not ask for reference to at least one religion.

SECTION I TEST

SECTION I: Believing in God

Answer both questions

1. a) What is natural evil? (2 marks)

   b) Do you think scientific explanations of the world show that God does not exist? Give two reasons for your point of view. (4 marks)

   c) Explain why the design argument leads some people to believe in God. (8 marks)

   d) 'Answered prayers prove that God exists.'
      (i) Do you agree? Give reasons for your opinion. (3 marks)
      (ii) Give reasons why some people may disagree with you. (3 marks)
      In your answer you should refer to at least one religion.

   (Total: 20 marks)

2. a) What is free will? (2 marks)

   b) Do you think that programmes or films about religion can affect a person's beliefs about God? Give two reasons for your point of view. (4 marks)

   c) Explain why religious experience may lead some people to believe in God. (8 marks)

   d) 'There is no evidence that God exists.'
      (i) Do you agree? Give reasons for your opinion. (3 marks)
      (ii) Give reasons why some people may disagree with you. (3 marks)
      In your answer you should refer to at least one religion.

   (Total: 20 marks)

You should now use the mark scheme in Appendix 1, page 98, to mark your answers, and the self-help tables in Appendix 1, pages 99–100, to see how you can improve your performance. If you need more help with the mark scheme for these questions, go to www.hoddereducation.co.uk/religionandlife

KEY WORDS FOR SECTION 2

Abortion	the removal of a foetus from the womb before it can survive
Assisted suicide	providing a seriously ill person with the means to commit suicide
Euthanasia	the painless killing of someone dying from a painful disease
Immortality of the soul	the idea that the soul lives on after the death of the body
Near-death experience	when someone about to die has an out of body experience
Non-voluntary euthanasia	ending someone's life painlessly when they are unable to ask, but you have good reason for thinking they would want you to do so
Paranormal	unexplained things which are thought to have spiritual causes, e.g. ghosts, mediums
Quality of life	the idea that life must have some benefits for it to be worth living
Reincarnation	the belief that, after death, souls are reborn in a new body
Resurrection	the belief that, after death, the body stays in the grave until the end of the world when it is raised
Sanctity of life	the belief that life is holy and belongs to God
Voluntary euthanasia	ending life painlessly when someone in great pain asks for death

Topic 2.1 Christian beliefs about life after death

Key points

Christians believe in life after death because:

- Jesus rose from the dead
- the Bible and the Creeds say there is life after death
- the Church teaches that there is life after death
- the soul is something that can never die.

Their beliefs about life after death affect their lives because Christians will try to love God and love their neighbour so that they go to heaven and not hell.

Evaluation questions

You may be asked to argue for and against Christian beliefs in life after death. For arguments for belief in life after death see 'Why Christians believe in life after death' on this page and for arguments against life after death see Topic 2.4, page 26.

Main points

Why Christians believe in life after death

All Christians believe in life after death because:

- The main Christian belief is that Jesus rose from the dead as this is what is recorded in the Gospels and New Testament. This proves there is life after death.
- St Paul teaches in 1 Corinthians that people will have a **resurrection** like that of Jesus.
- The major creeds of the Church teach that Jesus rose from the dead and that there will be life after death. Christians are supposed to believe the creeds and so they should believe in life after death.
- The Christian Churches teach that there is life after death.
- Many Christians believe in life after death because it gives their lives meaning and purpose. They feel that a life after death, in which people will be judged on how they live this life with the good rewarded and the evil punished, makes sense of this life.

How Christian beliefs about life after death affect the lives of Christians

- Christians believe that what happens to them after they die will be based on how they have lived this life. This means that Christians will try to live a good Christian life following the teachings of the Bible and the Church so that they go to heaven when they die.
- Living a good Christian life means loving God and loving your neighbour as yourself. So Christians' lives will be affected as they try to love God by praying every day and by worshipping God every Sunday.
- In the parable of the Sheep and Goats Jesus said Christians should feed the hungry, clothe the naked, befriend strangers, and visit the sick and those in prison. Jesus taught in the Good Samaritan that loving your neighbour means helping anyone in need. These teachings are bound to affect Christians' lives and explain why some Christians work for charities such as Christian Aid, CAFOD, etc.
- Christians believe that sin can prevent people from going to heaven. Indeed some Christians believe that those who die with unforgiven sins will go to hell. These beliefs mean that Christians will try to avoid committing sins in their lives so that they will go to heaven.

Topic 2.2.1 Islam and life after death

Main points

Why Muslims believe in life after death

Muslims believe in life after death because:

- The Qur'an teaches that there is life after death. Muslims believe that the Qur'an is the word of God and so its teachings must be true.
- Muhammad taught that there is life after death. Muslims believe that the Prophet Muhammad is the last prophet and the perfect example for Muslims so his teachings must be true.
- Belief in life after death is one of the six fundamental beliefs of Islam which all Muslims are expected to believe. So Muslims must believe in life after death.
- Muslims believe that this life is a test from God which must involve a judgement as to how they have done in the test, and rewards for those who pass. This can only happen if there is life after death.
- Many Muslims believe in life after death because it gives their lives meaning and purpose. They feel that for life to end at death does not make sense. Living your life in such a way that you spend eternity in heaven gives life meaning.

How Muslim beliefs about life after death affect the lives of Muslims

- Islam teaches that on the Last Day, all humans will be judged by God. Those who have lived good Muslim lives will go to paradise, everyone else will go to hell. This affects Muslims' lives because they must try to live good Muslim lives to avoid hell.
- Living a good Muslim life means keeping the Five Pillars of Islam (praying five times a day, fasting during Ramadan, paying zakah, going on hajj). So their beliefs about life after death will have a big effect on their lives.
- Living a good Muslim life also means eating halal food, observing Muslim dress laws, not drinking alcohol, not gambling nor being involved in lending at interest or receiving interest, etc.
- Muslim belief in resurrection means that nothing should be removed from the body after death. This affects Muslim lives because they try to avoid post-mortems and many Muslims have concerns about transplant surgery.
- Muslim beliefs about life after death give their lives meaning and purpose which may be why, in surveys, Muslims suffer less from depression than atheists and agnostics.

As you only need to study one religion, you should only learn one of the four topics on pages 21–24 – the religion you have studied at school.

Key points

- Muslims believe in life after death because it is taught in the Qur'an, in the hadith of the Prophet and is one of the essential six beliefs of Islam.
- Their beliefs about life after death affect their lives because Muslims will try to follow the Five Pillars and the teachings of the Shari'ah so that they go to heaven and not hell.

Evaluation questions

Evaluation questions will only ask you to refer to one religion, so you would be best just to use Christianity in answering evaluation questions, although you could use extra reasons from Islam.

Topic 2.2.2 Judaism and life after death

As you only need to study one religion, you should only learn one of the four topics on pages 21–24 – the religion you have studied at school.

Key points

- Jewish people believe in life after death because it is the teaching of the Tenakh and Talmud, and is one of the Thirteen Principles of Faith.
- Their beliefs about life after death affect their lives because Orthodox Jewish people will try to follow the halakhah so that they go to heaven and not hell.

Evaluation questions

Evaluation questions will only ask you to refer to one religion, so you would be best just to use Christianity in answering evaluation questions, although you could use extra reasons from Judaism.

Main points

Why Jewish people believe in life after death

Jewish people believe in life after death because:

- It is the teaching of the Tenakh which is inspired by God. Therefore Jews should believe what the Tenakh says.
- It is the teaching of the Talmud which most Jews try to follow because it is the teaching of rabbis.
- It is one of the Thirteen Principles of Faith which is part of the Jewish creed, and so should be believed.
- Many Jews believe in life after death because it gives their lives meaning and purpose. A life after death, in which people will be judged on how they live this life with the good rewarded and the evil punished, makes sense of this life.

How Jewish beliefs about life after death affect the lives of Jewish people

- Most Jews believe that God will decide what happens to people after they die on the basis of how they have lived their lives. This affects the lives of Jewish people because they must try to live good Jewish lives if they are to have a good life after death.
- Living a good Jewish life means observing the Torah and halakhah, praying three times a day, fasting on Yom Kippur, keeping Shabbat, celebrating the many festivals. Therefore their beliefs about life after death will have a big effect on their lives.
- Living a good Jewish life also means following all the mitzvot such as keeping kosher, observing the dress laws, and not being involved in lending at interest or receiving interest, etc.
- Orthodox Jews believe that they should confess their sins before they die, help with funerals and keep shiva. This affects their lives because they are always aware of death.
- Jewish beliefs about life after death give their lives meaning and purpose which may be why, in surveys, Jewish people suffer less from depression than atheists and agnostics.

Topic 2.2.3 Hinduism and life after death

Main points

Why Hindus believe in life after death

Hindus believe in life after death because:

- It is taught in the Vedas which contain eternal truths that most Hindus believe.
- It is taught in the Upanishads, which many Hindus also believe to contain eternal truths.
- It is taught in the Bhagavad Gita, and most Hindus feel that the teachings of the Gita contain ultimate truths and so must be believed.
- Many Hindus feel that for life to end at death does not make sense. They believe **reincarnation**, which rewards the good and punishes the evil when they die, makes sense of this life.
- Hindus also believe in life after death because of the evidence for reincarnation, for example children who are born knowing things they could not know unless they had been on Earth before.

How Hindu beliefs about life after death affect the lives of Hindus

- The aim of Hindu life is to escape from keep being reborn (samsara) through reaching moksha (freedom from rebirth) when the soul lives in paradise, often called nirvana. This affects the lives of Hindus because they must try to live the type of life that will lead them to moksha.
- The lives of some Hindus are very affected because they follow all the rules of the four stages of life (ashrama) in order to reach moksha.
- These Hindus believe in the law of karma and so they only do things in this life that will bring good effects in their next life.
- Some Hindus believe that the way to gain moksha is by devotion to Krishna, and spend a lot of time in worship (puja) both at home and in the mandir.
- Some Hindus believe that moksha is achieved through deep meditation to achieve oneness with Brahman (jnana yoga). This has a huge effect on their lives as they must live alone to spend sufficient time in meditation.

As you only need to study one religion, you should only learn one of the four topics on pages 21–24 – the religion you have studied at school.

Key points

- Hindus believe in life after death because it is the teaching of the Vedas, Upanishads and Gita.
- Their beliefs about life after death affect their lives because they will try to gain moksha either by living a good life, or living a life devoted to God or by living a life of meditation.

Evaluation questions

Evaluation questions will only ask you to refer to one religion, so you would be best just to use Christianity in answering evaluation questions, although you could use extra reasons from Hinduism.

Topic 2.2.4 Sikhism and life after death

As you only need to study one religion, you should only learn one of the four topics on pages 21–24 – the religion you have studied at school.

Key points

- Sikhs believe in life after death because it is the teaching of the Guru Granth Sahib and the Ten Gurus.
- Their beliefs about life after death affect their lives because they will try to gain mukti by living a good life which is God-centred.

Evaluation questions

Evaluation questions will only ask you to refer to one religion, so you would be best just to use Christianity in answering evaluation questions, although you could use extra reasons from Sikhism.

Main points

Why Sikhs believe in life after death

Sikhs believe in life after death because:

- It is taught in the Guru Granth Sahib which Sikhs regard as their living Guru and so must be believed. Many Sikhs regard the Guru Granth Sahib as the words of God.
- The Ten Gurus all believed in life after death and Sikhs should follow both the examples and the teachings of the human Gurus, and so should believe in life after death.
- Sikhs believe that God would not have created humans without a purpose. A good God is bound to have created a life after death for his creatures.
- Many Sikhs feel that for life to end at death does not make sense. They believe reincarnation, which rewards the good and punishes the evil when they die, makes sense of this life.
- Sikhs also believe in life after death because of the evidence for reincarnation such as children born knowing things they could not know unless they had been on Earth before.

How Sikh beliefs about life after death affect the lives of Sikhs

- Sikhism teaches that souls are reborn (samsara) until they are pure enough to reach mukti (release from rebirth) and the way to mukti is to move from being human-centred (manmukh) to being God-centred (gurmukh) and enter paradise. This is bound to affect a Sikh's life as they try to follow the Gurus' teachings on how to reach paradise.
- Following the Gurus' teachings involves abstaining from alcohol and drugs and only doing honest work, all of which affect a Sikh's life.
- To become gurmukh, a Sikh must give service to God, the gurdwara and other people. These are bound to affect a Sikh's life.
- Many Sikhs believe that to become gurmukh they must join the khalsa and wear the five Ks.

Topic 2.3 Non-religious reasons for believing in life after death

Main points

There are three main parts of the **paranormal** that provide non-religious reasons for believing in life after death.

1 Near-death experiences

This is when someone is clinically dead for a time and then comes back to life, and can remember what happened. Research by doctors in Britain, Holland and the USA has shown that about eight per cent of these cases have a **near-death experience**. The main features of these experiences are: feelings of peace; floating above the body; seeing a bright light; entering a heavenly place where they see dead relatives.

If near-death experiences are true, there must be life after death.

2 Evidence for a spirit world

Many people think of ghosts and ouija boards as evidence for a spirit world, but the clearest evidence comes from mediums. A medium is a person who claims to be able to communicate between our material world and a spirit world where the spirits of the dead live.

There are mediums in all countries and in all religions. They feature frequently on television channels such as Living TV. Most mediums claim that religious leaders like Jesus and Muhammad were in touch with the spirit world. They claim the spirit world gives people a second chance at life. Mediums contact people's dead relatives giving information they would not be able to without their contact being true. If mediums can contact the dead, there must be life after death.

3 The evidence of reincarnation

Hindus, Sikhs and Buddhists believe in reincarnation and have collected much evidence for this happening. If reincarnation is true, then there is life after death.

Key points

Some people believe in life after death for non-religious reasons such as:

- near-death experiences when people see things during heart attacks, operations, etc.
- evidence of the spirit world, ghosts, mediums, etc.
- evidence of reincarnation such as people remembering previous lives.

Evaluation questions

You may be asked to argue for and against the non-religious reasons for believing in life after death.

1. To argue for, you should use the reasons above.
2. To argue against, you could use these reasons:
   - Near-death experiences have been challenged by most scientists who claim they are simply products of the patient's brain as a result of chemical changes. Therefore there is no life after death.
   - The evidence from mediums is also very suspect. Many mediums have been proven to be frauds.

The only fool-proof test for mediums being true (set by Robert Thouless) has never been passed by a medium. So they do not prove there is life after death.

- Most beliefs about life after death think that the mind or soul can survive without the body, but science shows that the mind cannot live without the brain, so when the body dies, the mind must also die.

Topic 2.4 Why some people do not believe in life after death

Key points

Some people do not believe in life after death because:

- they do not believe in God
- there is no scientific evidence
- they do not see where life after death could take place.

Main points

Some people do not believe in God and believe this life is all there is. They do not believe in life after death because:

- If there is no God, there is no spirit world for life after death to happen.
- The different religions contradict each other about life after death. Christianity, Islam and Judaism say it will be resurrection or **immortality of the soul**; Hinduism, Sikhism and Buddhism say it will be reincarnation. If life after death were true, they would all say the same thing.
- Much of the evidence is based on holy books, but they contradict each other, and there is no way of deciding which holy books are true and which false.
- The evidence of the paranormal (near-death experiences, mediums, reincarnation) has all been challenged by scientists.
- Most beliefs about life after death think that the mind or soul can survive without the body, but science shows that the mind cannot live without the brain, so when the body dies, the mind must also die.
- There is no place where life after death could take place; space journeys have shown heaven is not above the sky.
- People who have been brought up by atheists will not believe in life after death.

Evaluation questions

You may be asked to argue for and against there being life after death, using evidence from at least one religion.

1. To argue for there being life after death, you should use the reasons why Christians believe in life after death (see Topic 2.1 page 20).

2. To argue against you should use the reasons above.

Topic 2.5 The nature of abortion

Main points

The law says that **abortion** is only allowed if two doctors agree:

- the mother's life is at risk
- the mother's physical or mental health is at risk
- the child is very likely to be born severely handicapped
- there would be a serious effect on other children in the family.

Abortions cannot be carried out after 24 weeks of pregnancy, unless the mother's life is at risk or the foetus has severe handicaps.

Why abortion is a controversial issue

Abortion is a controversial issue because:

- Many people believe that life begins at the moment of conception. Therefore abortion is taking a human life.
- Many people believe that life begins when the foetus is able to live outside the mother. Therefore abortion is not taking life.
- Many non-religious people believe that a woman should have the right to do what she wants with her own body. They might argue that an unwanted foetus is no different from an unwanted tumour.
- Many religious people believe that the unborn child's right to life is greater than the mother's rights.
- Some people argue the time limit should be reduced to 18 or 20 weeks because of medical advances.
- There are also arguments about whether medical staff should have to carry out abortions.

Key points

Abortion is allowed in the United Kingdom if two doctors agree that there is medical reason for it.

Abortion is a controversial issue because:

- people disagree about when life begins
- people disagree about whether abortion is murder
- people disagree about whether a woman has the right to choose.

Evaluation questions

Any evaluation questions are likely to ask you to refer to one religion, so the evaluation advice is after Topic 2.6 on page 28.

Topic 2.6 Christian attitudes to abortion

Key points

Christians have different attitudes to abortion:

- Some Christians believe that abortion is always wrong because it is murder and against God's will.
- Some Christians believe that abortion is wrong but must be allowed in some circumstances as the lesser of two evils.

Main points

Christians have two differing attitudes to abortion:

1. The Catholic Church and Evangelical Protestant Churches teach that all abortion (apart from medical treatments for the mother which affect the life of the foetus) is wrong whatever the circumstances because they believe that:
   - Life belongs to God, so only God has the right to end a pregnancy.
   - Life begins at conception so abortion is taking life and this is banned in the Ten Commandments.
   - They should follow the teaching of the Catholic Catechism (and Evangelical Protestant Churches) that all abortion is murder.
   - Counselling, help and adoption are alternatives to abortion for women made pregnant as a result of rape so that good can come out of evil in a new life.

2. Other Christians (mainly Liberal Protestants) disagree with abortion, but think it must be allowed in certain circumstances because they believe that:
   - Life does not begin at conception.
   - Jesus' command to love your neighbour means it is the duty of Christians to remove suffering, which abortion does.
   - The **sanctity of life** can be broken in such things as a just war, so why not in a just abortion?
   - If doctors have developed tests for certain medical conditions in unborn babies, parents should be allowed abortions if such tests show their baby would be born with serious medical problems.

Evaluation questions

You are likely to be asked one of two types of evaluation question about abortion:

1. One type will say something like: 'No Christian/religious person should ever have an abortion.' To answer this type of question you would use the reasons why some Christians think abortion is always wrong (part 1 of the main points) to argue for; and the reasons why some Christians allow abortion (part 2 of the main points) to argue against.

2. The other type will say something like: 'Every woman should have the right to an abortion if she wants one.' People who agree with this would use such reasons as:
   - Life does not begin at conception, it begins when the foetus is capable of surviving outside the womb on its own, so abortion is not the same as murder.
   - Abortion prevents a great deal of suffering. If babies are brought into the world with mothers who do not want them and cannot afford to bring them up, the babies will suffer, the mothers will suffer, and society will suffer in dealing with the situation.
   - A woman should have the right to do what she wants with her own body. They might argue that an unwanted foetus is no different from an unwanted tumour.

To argue against you should use the Christian reasons against abortion from part 1 of the main points above.

Topic 2.7.1 Islam and abortion

Main points

There are different attitudes to abortion among Muslims.

1 Many Muslims allow abortions up to 120 days of pregnancy for reasons such as the health of the mother or problems with the baby's health. The effect of having the baby on the present family can also be taken into consideration up to 120 days. They have this attitude because:
   - Some hadith say a foetus does not receive its soul until 120 days of pregnancy.
   - The Shari'ah says that the mother's life must always take priority.

2 Some Muslims believe that abortion should never be allowed. They believe this because:
   - They believe life begins at the moment of conception.
   - The Qur'an says murder is wrong and they think abortion is murder.
   - They believe that the Qur'an bans abortion.

3 Some Muslims believe that abortion can be allowed only if the mother's life is at risk. They believe this because:
   - The death of the unborn child is a lesser evil than the death of the mother and the Shari'ah says that the mother's life must always take priority.

As you only need to study one religion, you should only learn one of the four topics on pages 29–32 – the religion you have studied at school.

Key points

- Some Muslims think abortion should never be allowed.
- Some Muslims think abortion can only be allowed if the mother's life is in danger.
- Some Muslims think abortion is allowed until 120 days because this is when the foetus receives its soul.

Evaluation questions

Evaluation questions will only ask you to refer to one religion, so you would be best just to use Christianity in answering evaluation questions, although you could use extra reasons from Islam.

Topic 2.7.2 Judaism and abortion

As you only need to study one religion, you should only learn one of the four topics on pages 29–32 – the religion you have studied at school.

Key points

- Some Jews believe abortion is always wrong because life is in God's hands.
- Some Jews believe abortion can be allowed in certain circumstances because preventing avoidable suffering is taught in the Torah.

Evaluation questions

Evaluation questions will only ask you to refer to one religion, so you would be best just to use Christianity in answering evaluation questions, although you could use extra reasons from Judaism.

Main points

There are different attitudes to abortion in Judaism.

1 Some Jews believe that abortion can never be allowed because they believe:
   - Life begins at conception and so abortion is murder.
   - In the sanctity of life and so only God has the right to take life.

2 Many Jews believe that abortion is wrong, but if the mother's life is at risk, then it is permissible. They have this attitude because:
   - They believe in the sanctity of life and so think abortion is wrong.
   - The Torah permits killing in self-defence, and abortion is self-defence if the mother's life is at risk.

3 Some Jews believe in the UK law on abortion because:
   - They believe the Torah says that life does not begin until the foetus can survive on its own.
   - The Torah says that Jews must prevent avoidable suffering.
   - They believe the self-defence argument for abortion.

Topic 2.7.3 Hinduism and abortion

Main points

There are different attitudes to abortion in Hinduism.

1 Some Hindus believe that abortion is always wrong because:
   - Some Gurus have said that all abortion is wrong.
   - They believe that taking life gives bad karma.

2 Some Hindus believe that abortion should only be allowed if the mother's life is at risk because:
   - Hindu teachings on ahimsa say that violence can be used as a final choice.
   - If the foetus threatens the sanctity of the mother's life, abortion is acceptable.

3 Some British Hindus believe in the UK law on abortion because:
   - The teachings of the Gita mean that abortion will not affect karma as the soul of the foetus cannot be damaged.
   - They believe that life does not begin until the foetus can survive outside the womb.

As you only need to study one religion, you should only learn one of the four topics on pages 29–32 – the religion you have studied at school.

Key points

- Some Hindus think abortion should never be allowed.
- Some Hindus think abortion can only be allowed if the mother's life is in danger.
- Some Hindus think abortion is allowed in any circumstance.

Evaluation questions

Evaluation questions will only ask you to refer to one religion, so you would be best just to use Christianity in answering evaluation questions, although you could use extra reasons from Hinduism.

Topic 2.7.4 Sikhism and abortion

As you only need to study one religion, you should only learn one of the four topics on pages 29–32 – the religion you have studied at school.

Key points

- Many Sikhs believe abortion is wrong except for when the mother's life is at risk or she has been raped.
- Some Sikhs believe in the UK law on abortion because they believe sanctity of life involves removing suffering.

Evaluation questions

Evaluation questions will only ask you to refer to one religion, so you would be best just to use Christianity in answering evaluation questions, although you could use extra reasons from Sikhism.

Main points

There are different attitudes to abortion in Sikhism.

1 Some Sikhs believe that abortion can only be used if the mother's life is in danger or she has been raped because they believe:
- Life is sacred and begins at conception, so abortion is wrong.
- Only God has the right to take life.
- In the lesser of two evils; the death of the foetus is less evil than the death of the mother.

2 Some Sikhs allow abortion according to UK law. They have this attitude because:
- Sikhs regard each individual as important and a part of God's essence therefore the mother is more important than the child.
- They believe that sanctity of life involves more than just the baby (it involves the lives of the parents and siblings as well) and is also connected with the removal of suffering (babies which would suffer greatly if born).

Topic 2.8 The nature of euthanasia

Main points

Euthanasia is normally thought of as providing a gentle and easy death to someone suffering from a painful, deadly disease and who has little **quality of life**. This can be done by: **assisted suicide, voluntary euthanasia, non-voluntary euthanasia.**

British law says that all these methods of euthanasia are murder. However, the law now agrees that stopping artificial feeding or not giving treatment (often called passive euthanasia) are not euthanasia and so are lawful.

Why euthanasia is a controversial issue

1 Many people want euthanasia to remain illegal because
   - There is always likely to be doubt as to whether it is what the person really wants.
   - There is also the problem as to whether the disease will end the life; a cure might be found for the disease.
   - It is the job of doctors to save lives, not end them. Would patients trust doctors who kill their patients?
   - People might change their mind, but then it would be too late.
   - Who would check that it was only people who really wanted and needed euthanasia who died?

2 Many people want euthanasia to be made legal because:
   - Discoveries in medicine mean that people who would have died are being kept alive, often in agony, and should have the right to die.
   - Doctors have the right to switch off life-support machines if they think the patient has no chance of recovering, and allow people who have been in a coma for years to die. So euthanasia is already legal.
   - People have a right to commit suicide, so why not give them the right to ask doctors to assist their suicide if they are too weak to do it alone?
   - Just as doctors can now switch off life-support machines, so judges have said that doctors can stop treatment.

Evaluation questions

You may be asked to argue for and against the law on euthanasia being changed (this means euthanasia becoming legal).

1. The arguments for euthanasia becoming legal would come from part 2 above.

2. The arguments against would come from part 1 above.

33

Topic 2.9 Christian attitudes to euthanasia

Key points

All Christians are against euthanasia because they believe life is sacred and belongs to God. However, there are some different attitudes among Christians about switching off life-support machines, withdrawing treatment, etc. because some think these are not euthanasia.

Evaluation questions

You may be asked to argue for and against euthanasia referring to at least one religion.

1. The arguments for euthanasia should come from part 2 of Topic 2.8 (page 33).

2. The argument against could be that Christians are against euthanasia because:
   - The Bible bans suicide and voluntary euthanasia is a form of suicide.
   - All forms of euthanasia are murder, which is forbidden by the Ten Commandments.
   - Life is sacred and should only be taken by God. The Bible says that life and death decisions belong to God alone.

Main points

Although all Christians believe that euthanasia is wrong, there are slightly different attitudes:

1 Catholics and many Liberal Protestants believe that assisted suicide, voluntary euthanasia and non-voluntary euthanasia are all wrong. However, they believe that switching off life-support machines, not giving treatment that could cause distress, and giving dying people painkillers are not euthanasia. They have this attitude because:
   - They believe in the sanctity of life. Life is created by God and so it is up to God, not humans, when people die.
   - They regard euthanasia as murder, which is forbidden in the Ten Commandments.
   - If doctors say someone is brain-dead, then they have already died, so switching off the machine is accepting what God has already decided.
   - If you give painkillers to a dying person in great pain, and they kill the person, this is not murder because your intention was to remove their pain, not to kill them (doctrine of double effect).

2 Some Christians believe any form of euthanasia is wrong including switching off life-support machines, the refusal of extraordinary treatment, or the giving of large doses of painkillers. They have this attitude because:
   - They take the Bible teachings literally and the Bible forbids suicide.
   - Euthanasia includes switching off life-support machines, the refusal of extraordinary treatment, and giving large doses of painkillers because life is being ended by humans not God.
   - All forms of euthanasia are murder, which is banned by the Ten Commandments.
   - They believe that life is sacred and should only be taken by God. The Bible says that life and death decisions belong to God alone.

3 A few Christians accept euthanasia in certain circumstances because:
   - Medical advances mean it is hard to know what God's wishes about someone's death are. God may want someone to die but doctors are keeping them alive.
   - The teaching of Jesus on loving your neighbour can be used to justify assisting suicide, because it might be the most loving thing to do.
   - It is a basic human right to have control over your body and what people do to it. People have a right to refuse medical treatment, so why not a right to ask for euthanasia.

Topic 2.10.1 Islam and euthanasia

Main points

All Muslims are against euthanasia, but there are two slightly different attitudes.

1 Most Muslims are against all forms of euthanasia because:
   - The Qur'an bans suicide and so assisted suicide is wrong.
   - Most Muslims believe that voluntary euthanasia is just the same as assisted suicide.
   - Euthanasia is making yourself equal with God, which could be the greatest sin of shirk.
   - Euthanasia is murder, which is banned by the Qur'an.
   - Muslims believe life is a test from God and so if people use euthanasia, they are cheating in the test by trying to speed it up.

2 Some Muslims agree that euthanasia is wrong, but think switching off life-support machines is not euthanasia because:
   - Some Muslim lawyers have agreed to life-support machines being switched off when there are no signs of life.
   - If someone is brain-dead, God has already taken their life.

As you only need to study one religion, you should only learn one of the four topics on pages 35–38 – the religion you have studied at school.

Key points

All Muslims are against euthanasia because they believe life is sacred and belongs to God. However, there are some different attitudes among Muslims about the switching off of life-support machines, withdrawing treatment, etc. because some think these are not euthanasia.

Evaluation questions

Evaluation questions will only ask you to refer to one religion, so you would be best just to use Christianity in answering evaluation questions, although you could use extra reasons from Islam.

Topic 2.10.2 Judaism and euthanasia

As you only need to study one religion, you should only learn one of the four topics on pages 35–38 – the religion you have studied at school.

Key points

Jewish people are against euthanasia because they believe life is sacred and belongs to God. However, there are some different attitudes among Jewish people about switching off of life-support machines, withdrawing treatment, etc. because some think these are not euthanasia.

Evaluation questions

Evaluation questions will only ask you to refer to one religion, so you would be best just to use Christianity in answering evaluation questions, although you could use extra reasons from Judaism.

Main points

Judaism is against euthanasia, but there are two slightly different attitudes among Jewish people.

1 Many Jews do not allow euthanasia because:
- The Torah bans suicide and so assisted suicide is wrong.
- Most Jewish people believe that voluntary euthanasia is just the same as assisted suicide.
- Murder is banned by the Ten Commandments and euthanasia is a form of murder.
- The Tenakh says that death and life are in the hands of God.

2 Some Jews believe euthanasia is wrong but accept switching off life-support machines or not 'striving to keep alive'. They believe this because:
- Some rabbis have said switching off life-support for the brain-dead is not euthanasia.
- If someone is brain-dead, God has already taken their life.
- Striving to keep someone alive is preventing God from taking their soul and so is against God's wishes.

Topic 2.10.3 Hinduism and euthanasia

Main points

There are different attitudes to euthanasia in Hinduism.

1 Some Hindus are against all forms of euthanasia because:
   - The teaching on ahimsa means that euthanasia is unacceptable because it must involve inflicting violence.
   - Euthanasia would damage a soul and bring bad karma, stopping the soul from gaining moksha.
   - According to the law of karma, God alone must give and take life at the right time.
   - The Laws of Manu say that murder is wrong.

2 Some Hindus believe that euthanasia can be allowed in certain circumstances. They accept switching off of life-support machines and not striving to keep someone alive and also believe euthanasia should be allowed when there is no quality of life. They have this attitude because:
   - If someone is brain-dead, God has already taken their life and so switching off the life-support machine would not be euthanasia.
   - The Gita teaches that the soul cannot be harmed.
   - Refusing euthanasia when there is no quality of life is a form of violence and so is against ahimsa.
   - Striving to keep someone alive is preventing the soul from moving on to moksha or its next life.

As you only need to study one religion, you should only learn one of the four topics on pages 35–38 – the religion you have studied at school.

Key points

- Some Hindus agree with euthanasia if the dying person wants to die easily because it releases the soul.
- Other Hindus only allow life-support machines to be switched off and no other form of euthanasia because life is sacred.

Evaluation questions

Evaluation questions will only ask you to refer to one religion, so you would be best just to use Christianity in answering evaluation questions, although you could use extra reasons from Hinduism.

Topic 2.10.4 Sikhism and euthanasia

As you only need to study one religion, you should only learn one of the four topics on pages 35–38 – the religion you have studied at school.

Key points

- Most Sikhs are against euthanasia because they believe life and death should be in the hands of God, and that killing brings bad karma and so will prevent mukti.
- Some Sikhs accept not striving to keep someone alive and switching off of life-support machines because not to do so would prevent the release of the soul.

Evaluation questions

Evaluation questions will only ask you to refer to one religion, so you would be best just to use Christianity in answering evaluation questions, although you could use extra reasons from Sikhism.

Main points

Sikhism is against euthanasia, but there are two slightly different attitudes among Sikh people.

1 Most Sikhs are against all forms of euthanasia because:
- Sikh teaching on violence to humans means that euthanasia would bring bad karma and prevent mukti.
- According to the law of karma, God alone must give and take life at the right time.
- The Rahit Maryada says that murder is wrong.
- Euthanasia would be damaging a soul, which is condemned in the Guru Granth Sahib.
- To practise euthanasia is making oneself equal to God, the worst form of manmukh, and would create a massive amount of bad karma.

2 Many Sikhs are against euthanasia but allow the switching off of life-support machines and not striving to keep alive because:
- If someone is brain-dead their life has already ended, so it is not being taken.
- Striving to keep someone alive is preventing the soul from moving on, so it is stopping the law of karma.
- Release of the soul is the aim of Sikh life, so people should not be kept alive artificially.

Topic 2.11 The media and matters of life and death

Main points

The media are all forms of communication, including newspapers, television, radio, films and the internet. Remember that the word is plural.

1 Arguments that the media should not be free to criticise what religions say about matters of life and death

- Some people believe that criticising what religions say on matters of life and death is a way of stirring up religious hatred, which is banned by the Racial and Religious Hatred Act of 2007. For example, when the Catholic Church told Catholics to withdraw their support from Amnesty International because Amnesty had decided abortion should be a human right for women who had been raped, the media reports chose examples that showed the Catholic position in a bad light.
- Many religious believers believe the freedom of the media should be limited because of the offence criticism of religious attitudes can bring. For example, when a Danish newspaper published cartoons of the Prophet Muhammad in 2006, there were riots in some countries.
- Some religious believers believe that criticising what religious leaders say about matters of life and death is close to the crime of blasphemy. If the media criticise the Pope's teachings on a topic like abortion, they are condemning the Catholic Church.
- Some religious people feel that religious statements are based on what God says and so are beyond human criticism.

2 Arguments that the media should be free to criticise what religions say about matters of life and death

- Freedom of expression is a basic human right which is needed for democracy to work. Before people vote they need to know what is going on in the world and in their own country. For this they need a free media, and if the media have freedom of expression, then they must be free to criticise religious attitudes to matters of life and death.
- If religious leaders use the media to make statements about matters of life and death (as they do on things like stem-cell research), they must be prepared for the media to criticise those statements.
- In a multi-faith society such as the UK, there must be freedom of religious belief and expression. This means that the media must have the right to question and even criticise not only religious beliefs, but also what religions say about life and death issues.
- Life and death issues are so important to everyone that people want to know what is the right view. This could not be done if religions were allowed to put forward views that no one could criticise.

Key points

Some people think that what religions say about matters of life and death should not be criticised by the media because:

- they might stir up religious hatred
- they might be offensive to religious believers.

Other people think the media should be free to criticise religious attitudes because:

- a free media is a key part of democracy
- if religions want to be free to say what they want, then the media must be free to criticise religion.

Evaluation questions

You may be asked to argue for and against the media being free to criticise religious attitudes to matters of life and death.

1. You should use the arguments that the media should be free from point 2 on the left.

2. You should use the arguments that the media should not be free from point 1 on the left.

How to answer questions on Section 2

You should already know the basics about how to answer questions from Section 1, pages 15–17, but here is an answer to a whole question on section 2 with a commentary to help you.

Question a)
What is resurrection? (2 marks)

Answer

Coming back to life.

> One mark for a partially correct answer.

Answer

The belief that, after death, the body stays in the grave until the end of the world when it is raised.

> Two marks for a correct definition.

Question b)
Do you think euthanasia should be allowed? Give TWO reasons for your point of view. (4 marks)

Answer

I do not think euthanasia should be allowed because euthanasia is murder …

> One mark for a reason.

… which is banned in the Qur'an.

> Two marks because the reason is developed.

Also euthanasia is making yourself equal with Allah …

> Three marks because a second reason is given.

… which could be the greatest sin of shirk.

> Four marks because the second reason is developed.

> Total = four marks. Remember! Response questions are really like part (i) of an evaluation question where you only have to give two reasons. To answer a response question, you should just use two reasons from the point of view you agree with in the evaluation questions advice for a topic.

Question c)
Choose one religion other than Christianity and explain why some of its followers agree with abortion and some do not. (8 marks)

Answer

Many Muslims allow abortions up to 120 days of pregnancy because some hadith say a foetus does not receive its soul until 120 days of pregnancy.

> LEVEL 1: two marks for a reason for one attitude expressed in basic English.

Also the Shari'ah says that the mother's life must always take priority and so abortion must be allowed if the mother's life is at risk.

> LEVEL 2: by giving a second reason for the attitude, the answer goes up to level 2 and because the answer is written in clear English it would gain four marks.

Some Muslims believe that abortion should never be allowed because they believe life begins at the moment of conception and therefore abortion is murder.

> LEVEL 3: by adding another attitude with a reason the answer moves up to level 3 and because the answer is written in a clear style of English with some use of specialist vocabulary (hadith, Shari'ah, moment of conception) it would gain six marks.

The Qur'an says murder is wrong and they believe the Qur'an is the word of God.

Therefore if abortion is banned and murder is banned by the Qur'an, no Muslim should have an abortion.

> LEVEL 4: by adding a further reason for the second attitude, the answer moves up to level 4 and because it is written in a clear and correct style of English with more specialist vocabulary (Qur'an, word of God, banned, Muslim) it would gain eight marks – full marks.

Question d)

'There is no evidence for life after death.'

(i) Do you agree? Give reasons for your opinion. (3 marks)
(ii) Give reasons why some people may disagree with you. (3 marks)

In your answer, you should refer to at least one religion.

Answer

(i) I do agree because I am an atheist, and if there is no God, there can be no life after death.

| One mark for a personal opinion with a reason. |

The main evidence for life after death is based on holy books, but how do we know they are true? They contradict each other (e.g. the Qur'an says there will be resurrection, the Gita says there will be reincarnation) and there is no way of deciding which holy books are true and which false.

| Another reason is given so it moves up to two marks. |

Finally, there is no place where life after death could take place; space journeys have shown heaven is not above the sky. If there is nowhere for life after death to take place, there cannot be a life after death.

| The answer now gives another reason for the opinion, so it moves up to three marks. |

(ii) Christians would disagree with me because they believe that Jesus rising from the dead proves there is life after death.

| One mark for a reason why some people might disagree. |

The Bible and all the Christian Churches teach that there is life after death. Protestant, Catholic, Orthodox and Pentecostal Churches may have some differences about what they think life after death will be like, but they all teach their followers that there will be life after death.

| Another reason is given so it moves up to two marks. |

Many religious believers think there must be a life after death to make sense of this life. They feel there must be a life after death in which people will be judged on how they have lived this life so that the good are rewarded and the evil are punished.

| The answer now gives another reason for some people disagreeing, so it moves up to three marks. |

| This answer to question d) can gain full marks because part (i) refers to Islam and Hinduism and part (ii) refers to Christianity. |

SECTION 2 TEST

SECTION 2: Matters of life and death

Answer both questions

1. a) What is quality of life? (2 marks)

   b) Do you think there is life after death? Give two reasons for your point of view (4 marks)

   c) Explain how their beliefs about life after death affect the lives of Christians. (8 marks)

   d) 'Religious people should never have abortions.'
      (i) Do you agree? Give reasons for your opinion. (3 marks)
      (ii) Give reasons why some people may disagree with you. (3 marks)
      In your answer, you should refer to at least one religion.

   (Total: 20 marks)

2. a) What is immortality of the soul? (2 marks)

   b) Do you think the media should be free to criticise what religion says about matters of life and death? Give two reasons for your point of view. (4 marks)

   c) Choose one religion other than Christianity and explain why its followers believe in life after death. (8 marks)

   d) 'Everyone should have the right to euthanasia if they have no quality of life.'
      (i) Do you agree? Give reasons for your opinion. (3 marks)
      (ii) Give reasons why some people may disagree with you. (3 marks)
      In your answer you should refer to at least one religion.

   (Total: 20 marks)

You should now use the mark scheme in Appendix 1, page 98, to mark your answers, and the self-help tables in Appendix 1, pages 99–100, to see how you can improve your performance. If you need more help with the mark scheme for these questions, go to www.hoddereducation.co.uk/religionandlife

Section 3 Marriage and the family

KEY WORDS FOR SECTION 3

Adultery	a sexual act between a married person and someone other than their marriage partner
Civil partnership	a legal ceremony giving a homosexual couple the same legal rights as a husband and wife
Cohabitation	living together without being married
Contraception	intentionally preventing pregnancy from occurring
Faithfulness	staying with your marriage partner and having sex only with them
Homosexuality	sexual attraction to the same sex
Nuclear family	mother, father and children living as a unit
Pre-marital sex	sex before marriage
Procreation	making a new life
Promiscuity	having sex with a number of partners without commitment
Re-constituted family	where two sets of children (step-brothers and step-sisters) become one family when their divorced parents marry each other
Re-marriage	marrying again after being divorced from a previous marriage

Topic 3.1 Changing attitudes to marriage and family life

Key points

- Fifty years ago, most people only had sex in marriage, and they married in church. Now, people have sex before they marry, cohabitation is acceptable and most marriages are not in church. This could be caused by safer contraception and fewer people being influenced by religion.
- Divorce and re-marriage used to be rare and people were looked down on if they divorced. Today, divorce and re-marriage are accepted, and two in five marriages end in divorce. The changes may have been caused by cheaper divorce and women having more equality.
- Family life has changed so that, although most children are still brought up by a mother and a father, the parents may not be married or they may have been married more than once. These changes are probably caused by the changing attitudes to sex, marriage and divorce.
- Homosexuality used to be illegal, but now homosexuals have the same rights to sexual activity as heterosexuals including civil partnerships. These changes are probably due to discoveries showing that homosexuality is natural and to changes to the law.

Main points

In the UK in the 1960s, it was expected that young people only had sex after marriage; most married young, in church, for life; families were husband and wife and children (**nuclear family**); and male **homosexuality** was a criminal offence.

How attitudes have changed

- Most people have sex before marriage.
- Many couples live together (cohabit) rather than marry.
- The average age for marrying has increased.
- Most marriages do not take place in church.
- Divorce is accepted as a normal part of life.
- There is much more divorce and so more single-parent families and **re-constituted families**.
- There are more extended families as more mothers are in paid employment.
- There are many more single-parent families as more couples divorce.
- More children are being brought up by cohabiting parents.
- Society treats homosexual sex the same way as heterosexual sex.
- Two people of the same sex can now form a legal union by signing a registration document in a **civil partnership**, giving them the same rights and treatment as an opposite-sex married couple.

Reasons for the changes

Cohabitation and marriage

- Effective **contraception** made it safer to have sex before marriage.
- Fewer people went to church and so were not encouraged to keep sex until after marriage.
- The media and celebrities made **cohabitation** look respectable and so it became more popular.
- The media showed sexual relationships outside of marriage as the norm so more people thought sex outside marriage was acceptable.

Divorce

- New laws made divorce much cheaper and easier for ordinary people.
- Increased equality for women means that women are no longer prepared to accept unequal treatment from men, and if their husbands treat them badly, they will divorce them.
- Most married women depended on their husband's wages, but now many women are financially independent and can support themselves after a divorce.
- There has been a great change in how long people are likely to be married. Most divorces occur after ten years of marriage, which was the average length of a marriage 100 years ago.

Family life

- The popularity of cohabitation means there are more families where the parents are not married.
- The increase in divorce has led to an increase in **re-marriage** and so there are now many more re-constituted families.
- More mothers are in paid employment and use retired grandparents or close relatives to look after their children.
- The increase in divorce and the acceptance of unmarried mothers means there are more single-parent families.

Homosexuality

- Changes in the laws have made it easier to be openly homosexual and made society more aware of homosexuality.
- Medical research has shown that homosexuality is natural, leading people to accept equal status and rights for homosexual couples.
- Media coverage of gay celebrities has led to a greater acceptance of all gay people.
- The work of gay rights organisations has led to a greater acceptance of equal rights for homosexuals.

Evaluation questions

Evaluation questions are likely to ask you to refer to at least one religion so the advice on evaluation questions is after Topic 3.2 on page 46.

Topic 3.2 Christian attitudes to sex outside marriage

Key points

- All Christians believe adultery is wrong as it breaks one of the Ten Commandments.
- Most Christians believe that sex before marriage is wrong because the Church and the Bible teach this.

Main points

Most Christians believe sex outside marriage is wrong because:

- God gave us sex for the **procreation** of children who should be brought up in a Christian family, so sex should only take place within a marriage.
- The Bible says that sex outside of marriage is sinful and Christians should follow the teachings of the Bible.
- The Catechism says that **pre-marital sex** is wrong and Catholics should follow the teachings of the Catechism.
- All Christians are against **adultery** because it breaks the wedding vows.
- Adultery is also banned by the Ten Commandments, which all Christians should follow.
- Adultery is condemned by Jesus and all Christians should follow the teachings of Jesus.

Some Christians accept that couples may live together before marriage, but only in a long-term relationship leading to marriage.

Evaluation questions

You are likely to be asked to argue for and against allowing sex before marriage.

1. People who agree with sex before marriage are likely to use such reasons as:
   - Sex is a natural result of two people being in love, and there is no reason for them waiting until they are married.
   - Modern contraception means that a couple can have sex without the risk of pregnancy, so unwanted children are not likely to result from sex before marriage.
   - Sex before marriage is now accepted by society and very few people think it is wrong.

2. Most Christians disagree with sex before marriage and so would use the reasons in the main points above.

You may also be asked to argue for and against getting married rather than living together.

1. Christians believe marriage is better than living together because:
   - Marriage is God's gift (a sacrament for many Christians), the way God says humans should have sex and bring up a family.

- The Bible teaches that sex should only take place in marriage and that marriage is necessary for the upbringing of a Christian family.
- The Church teaches that marriage is the basis of society and that living together without marriage is wrong.
- Statistics show that married couples are more likely to stay together than cohabiting couples and that the children of married couples have a more stable and happy life.

2. People who believe living together is as good as marriage give such reasons as:
   - Couples who live together can be just as happy and committed as those who marry.
   - You cannot promise to stay with someone until death if you do not know what it will be like to live with them.
   - Living together brings all the commitment and joy of marriage without the legal complications.
   - Weddings are expensive and living together allows a couple to spend that money on the home, children, etc.

Topic 3.3.1 Islam and sex outside marriage

Main points

Muslims believe that sex outside of marriage is wrong because:

- Sex before marriage is forbidden by the Qur'an, and Muslims believe the Qur'an is the word of God.
- The Shari'ah says that sex should only take place in marriage.
- Islam teaches that sex is for the procreation of children who should be raised in a family where the mother and father are married.
- Adultery is condemned by God in the Qur'an.
- Adultery breaks the marriage contract that both husband and wife have agreed to.
- Adultery is likely to harm the family, and harming the family is condemned by both the Qur'an and Shari'ah.

As you only need to study one religion, you should only learn one of the four topics on pages 47–50 – the religion you have studied at school.

Key points

Muslims believe that sex before marriage and adultery are wrong because the Qur'an teaches this.

Evaluation questions

Evaluation questions will only ask you to refer to one religion, so you would be best just to use Christianity in answering evaluation questions, although you could use extra reasons from Islam.

Topic 3.3.2 Judaism and sex outside marriage

As you only need to study one religion, you should only learn one of the four topics on pages 47–50 – the religion you have studied at school.

Key points

- All Jews believe adultery is wrong as it breaks one of the Ten Commandments.
- Most Jews believe that sex before marriage is wrong because the Torah teaches this.
- Some Jews believe that sex before marriage can be accepted with certain conditions.

Evaluation questions

Evaluation questions will only ask you to refer to one religion, so you would be best just to use Christianity in answering evaluation questions, although you could use extra reasons from Judaism.

Main points

Jewish people believe that sex outside of marriage is wrong because:

- Sex before marriage is forbidden by the Torah, which all Jewish people should follow.
- The Talmud says that sex should only take place in marriage, so Jewish people should avoid sex outside marriage.
- Judaism teaches that sex is for the procreation of children who should be raised in a family where the mother and father are married.
- Adultery is banned by the Ten Commandments, which all Jewish people should follow.
- Adultery breaks the marriage contract that both husband and wife have agreed to.
- Adultery is likely to harm the family, which should not be harmed as it is where children learn about Judaism and how to live the Jewish life.

Some Progressive Jews accept that couples may live together before marriage, but only in a long-term relationship leading to marriage.

Topic 3.3.3 Hinduism and sex outside marriage

Main points

Hindus believe that sex outside of marriage is wrong because:

- Sex is not allowed in the student stage of life (ashrama), so sex before marriage would prevent you from gaining moksha.
- The Hindu scriptures say that sex should only take place in marriage.
- Hinduism teaches that sex is for the procreation of children who should be raised in a family where the mother and father are married.
- Committing adultery is betraying your dharma, which prevents your soul from achieving moksha.
- Adultery is a betrayal of the marriage partner and betrayal brings bad karma.
- Adultery is likely to harm the family, which should not be harmed as it is where children learn to be good Hindus.

As you only need to study one religion, you should only learn one of the four topics on pages 47–50 – the religion you have studied at school.

Key points

Hindus believe that sex before marriage and adultery are wrong because sex is only allowed in the householder stage of life and adultery brings bad karma.

Evaluation questions

Evaluation questions will only ask you to refer to one religion, so you would be best just to use Christianity in answering evaluation questions, although you could use extra reasons from Hinduism.

Topic 3.3.4 Sikhism and sex outside marriage

As you only need to study one religion, you should only learn one of the four topics on pages 47–50 – the religion you have studied at school.

Key points

Sikhs believe that sex outside marriage is wrong. Sex before marriage is banned by the Rahit Maryada. Adultery breaks the sacred marriage union.

Evaluation questions

Evaluation questions will only ask you to refer to one religion, so you would be best just to use Christianity in answering evaluation questions, although you could use extra reasons from Sikhism.

Main points

Sikhs believe that sex outside of marriage is wrong because:

- The Gurus did not have sex before marriage and all Sikhs should follow their examples.
- The Rahit Maryada says there should be no sex before marriage.
- Marriages are usually arranged by families. Having sex before marriage would make this more difficult.
- Adultery is breaking the marriage union and would be manmukh behaviour making attaining mukti more difficult.
- Adultery is forbidden by the Rahit Maryada.
- All the human Gurus were faithful husbands who never committed adultery, and all Sikhs should follow their examples.
- Adultery is likely to harm the family, which should not be harmed as it is where children learn to be good Sikhs.

Topic 3.4 Christian attitudes to divorce

Main points

There are two different attitudes to divorce in Christianity:

1 The Catholic Church does not allow religious divorce or re-marriage. The only way a marriage between baptised Catholics can be ended is by the death of one of the partners.

However, the Catholic Church does allow civil divorce if that will be better for the children, but the couple are still married in the eyes of God and so cannot re-marry. Catholics have this attitude because:

- Jesus taught that divorce is wrong and Christians should follow his teachings.
- The couple have made a covenant with God which 'cannot be broken by any earthly power'.
- The Catechism teaches that a marriage cannot be dissolved and so religious divorce is impossible.
- There can be no re-marriage as there can be no religious divorce, so re-marriage would be both bigamy (having two husbands or wives) and adultery.

However, if it can be proved that the marriage was never a true Christian marriage, Catholics can have an annulment which makes them free to re-marry.

2 Most non-Catholic Churches think that divorce is wrong, but allow it if the marriage has broken down and permit divorced people to remarry. They are sometimes asked to promise that this time their marriage will be for life.

Non-Catholic Churches allow divorce because:

- Jesus allowed divorce in Matthew 19:9 for a partner's adultery.
- If a marriage has really broken down then the effects of the couple not divorcing would be a greater evil than the evil of divorce itself ('the lesser of two evils').
- If Christians repent and confess their sins they can be forgiven; this means a couple should have another chance at marriage if they are keen to make it work this time.
- These Churches believe it is better to divorce than to live in hatred and quarrel all the time.

Key points

- Catholics do not allow religious divorce and re-marriage because they believe the marriage vows cannot be broken.
- Other Christians disapprove of divorce, but allow religious divorce and re-marriage if the marriage has broken down, because Christianity teaches forgiveness.

Evaluation questions

For arguments in favour of divorce use the non-Catholic reasons for allowing divorce in the second main point. For arguments against divorce use the Catholic reasons for not allowing divorce in the first main point.

Topic 3.5.1 Islam and divorce

As you only need to study one religion, you should only learn one of the four topics on pages 52–55 – the religion you have studied at school.

Key points

- Most Muslims allow divorce because it is permitted by the Qur'an.
- Some Muslims do not allow divorce because Muhammad said God disapproves of it.

Evaluation questions

Evaluation questions will only ask you to refer to one religion, so you would be best just to use Christianity in answering evaluation questions, although you could use extra reasons from Islam.

Main points

Divorce and re-marriage are allowed in Islam, but there are different attitudes.

1 Some Muslims would not divorce because:
- Muhammad is reported to have said that divorce is the most hated of lawful things and they follow what Muhammad said.
- Most marriages are arranged by families, so there is family pressure against divorce.
- Many Muslims believe they will be sent to hell if they harm their children, and divorce is likely to harm the children.
- The Qur'an teaches that families should try to rescue the marriage before they divorce.

2 Most Muslims believe that divorce should be allowed because:
- The Qur'an permits divorce and sets out the terms for custody of children and care for divorced wives.
- The Shari'ah permits divorce and has many laws about how divorce and re-marriage should operate.
- Most Muslims believe divorce is a lesser evil than forcing a couple to live in hatred and bitterness.
- Marriage is a contract in Islam and the contract says what is to happen if the couple divorce so divorce must be allowed.

Topic 3.5.2 Judaism and divorce

Main points

There are three different attitudes to divorce among Jewish people.

1 Some Jewish people believe that divorce is wrong because:
   - The Talmud teaches that divorce is an offence to God, and they follow the Talmud teachings.
   - Children need to be brought up as good followers of Judaism for the faith to survive, and divorce may stop this.
   - Some rabbis have taught that divorce is wrong because of the harm it can cause for the family if only one partner wants a divorce, or if there are likely to be financial problems.

2 Most Orthodox Jews allow divorce but only if the husband has a get from the Bet Din because:
   - The Torah has various statements that permit divorce.
   - Marriage in Judaism is a contract that can be broken in certain circumstances.
   - The halakhah says that only men can apply to the Bet Din for a get.

3 Most Reform Jews allow divorce and allow both men and women to apply for a get from the Bet Din because:
   - They believe that the Torah and halakhah need interpreting to fit modern life.
   - They believe that men and women should have equal rights in religion and also in divorce.
   - They believe divorce is a lesser evil than forcing a couple to live in hatred and bitterness.

As you only need to study one religion, you should only learn one of the four topics on pages 52–55 – the religion you have studied at school.

Key points

- Some Jewish people are against divorce because of the teachings of the Talmud and rabbis.
- Orthodox Jews allow divorce, but give special rights to men in divorce because of the Torah.
- Reform Jews allow divorce, but give equal divorce rights to women because they think the Torah should be brought up to date.

Evaluation questions

Evaluation questions will only ask you to refer to one religion, so you would be best just to use Christianity in answering evaluation questions, although you could use extra reasons from Judaism.

Topic 3.5.3 Hinduism and divorce

As you only need to study one religion, you should only learn one of the four topics on pages 52–55 – the religion you have studied at school.

Key points

- Some Hindus do not allow divorce because they believe marriage is for life.
- Many Hindus allow divorce especially if the couple cannot have children because they think arguing and quarrelling in a marriage will give bad karma.

Evaluation questions

Evaluation questions will only ask you to refer to one religion, so you would be best just to use Christianity in answering evaluation questions, although you could use extra reasons from Hinduism.

Main points

There are different attitudes to divorce among Hindus, but all Hindus believe divorced couples can re-marry.

1 Traditional Hindus believe that there should be no divorce, unless the couple are childless after fifteen years or if there is cruelty. They have this attitude because:
   - It is the teaching of the Laws of Manu.
   - Divorce is likely to harm families and so should be discouraged.
   - Having children is part of your duty as a householder so childlessness is grounds for divorce.
   - Violence in marriage is against ahimsa and so would be grounds for divorce.

2 Many other Hindus believe that divorce should be allowed if a marriage has broken down because:
   - They regard the Laws of Manu as out of date.
   - Some Gurus and swamis teach that divorce is acceptable for Hindus.
   - Living in hatred and discord brings bad karma, so divorce would be needed for the soul to gain moksha.
   - They believe divorce is a lesser evil than forcing a couple to live in hatred and bitterness.

Topic 3.5.4 Sikhism and divorce

Main points

All Sikhs believe that marriage should be for life, but there are different attitudes to divorce.

1   Most Sikhs believe that there should be no divorce because:
    *   Two souls are united in a Sikh marriage, and they should not be split by divorce.
    *   None of the Gurus divorced, and Sikhs should follow the example of the Gurus.
    *   The Rahit Maryada disapproves of divorce and all good Sikhs should follow the guidance of the Rahit Maryada.
    *   As Sikh marriages are often arranged, there are family pressures against divorce.

2   Some Sikhs believe that divorce should be allowed if a marriage has broken down because:
    *   They follow the culture of the Punjab where divorce is common.
    *   If a couple live in hatred and discord they will gather bad karma, but divorce might allow the soul to gain mukti.
    *   They believe divorce is a lesser evil than forcing a couple to live in hatred and bitterness.

As you only need to study one religion, you should only learn one of the four topics on pages 52–55 – the religion you have studied at school.

Key points

*   Some Sikhs believe there should be no divorce because marriage is for life and the Gurus did not divorce.
*   Other Sikhs allow divorce because living in hatred will bring bad karma and prevent mukti.

Evaluation questions

Evaluation questions will only ask you to refer to one religion, so you would be best just to use Christianity in answering evaluation questions, although you could use extra reasons from Sikhism.

Topic 3.6 Why family life is important for Christians

Key points

Christians believe that the family is important because:

- it is taught in the Bible
- Christian marriage services refer to bringing up a family as one of the main purposes of marriage
- Christians believe that the family was created by God.

Main points

Family life is important for Christians because:

- One of the main purposes of Christian marriage is to have children and bring them up in a Christian environment so that they become good Christians.
- Christianity teaches that the family was created by God as the basis of society and the only place for the upbringing of children.
- Christian teaching on divorce shows that the family is too important to be broken up by divorce.
- Without the family, children would not learn the difference between right and wrong.
- The family is very important for Christianity to continue and grow as it is the family that brings children into the faith.

However, Jesus taught that there are more important things than the family which is why Catholic priests, nuns and monks leave their families so that they can serve God.

Evaluation questions

You may be asked to argue for and against family life being more important for religious than non-religious people.

1. You could use any of the main points above for family life being more important for Christians than non-religious people.

2. Arguments against family life being more important for religious than non-religious people:
   - Many non-religious people see their family as being the most important thing in their lives, whereas many religious people see their religion as more important than their family.
   - Most non-religious people have just as good a family life as religious people.
   - Non-religious families can respect their children more because they do not have to force them to try to be religious.
   - Religion cannot make a difference to how much parents love their children, and children love their parents.

Topic 3.7.1 Islam and family life

Main points

Family life is important in Islam because:

- Muslim parents will be judged by God on how well they have brought up their children. If family life decides whether Muslims go to heaven, it must be very important.
- The Qur'an teaches that the family was created by God as the basic unit of society and as the only place in which children should be brought up.
- The Prophet Muhammad married and raised a family, so Muslims must marry and raise a family.
- Without the family, children would not learn the difference between right and wrong.
- The family is very important for Islam to continue and grow as it is the family that brings children into the faith.

As you only need to study one religion, you should only learn one of the four topics on pages 57–60 – the religion you have studied at school.

Key points

Family life is important in Islam because the Qur'an says that the family is the basis of society and Muslims should follow the example of Muhammad who raised a family.

Evaluation questions

Evaluation questions will only ask you to refer to one religion, so you would be best just to use Christianity in answering evaluation questions, although you could use extra reasons from Islam.

Topic 3.7.2 Judaism and family life

As you only need to study one religion, you should only learn one of the four topics on pages 57–60 – the religion you have studied at school.

Main points

Family life is important in Judaism because:

- It is a mitzvot for Jewish people to marry and have children, and obeying the mitzvot is an essential part of being Jewish.
- Only children of married Jewish parents are automatically Jewish, so the family is very important for the continuation of the Jewish people and religion.
- Without the family, children would not learn the difference between right and wrong.
- The family is the place where Shabbat is observed and the festivals are celebrated.
- The importance of family life is commanded in the fifth of the Ten Commandments.

Key points

Family life is important in Judaism because the family is the only way of keeping Judaism alive and the Torah says all Jews should marry and raise a family.

Evaluation questions

Evaluation questions will only ask you to refer to one religion, so you would be best just to use Christianity in answering evaluation questions, although you could use extra reasons from Judaism.

Topic 3.7.3 Hinduism and family life

Main points

Family life is important in Hinduism because:

- Unless Hindus perform their duties as a householder and raise a family, they will not achieve moksha. So the family is important as the way to reach nirvana.
- Hinduism teaches that the family was created by God as the basic unit of society and as the only place in which children should be brought up.
- Without the family, children would not learn the difference between right and wrong.
- The family is very important for Hinduism to continue and grow as it is the family that brings children into the faith.
- The Hindu scriptures show the importance of Hindu family life and Hindus should follow the guidance of the scriptures.

As you only need to study one religion, you should only learn one of the four topics on pages 57–60 – the religion you have studied at school.

Key points

Family life is important in Hinduism because Hinduism teaches that the family is the basis of society and raising a family is part of the dharma of the householder stage of life.

Evaluation questions

Evaluation questions will only ask you to refer to one religion, so you would be best just to use Christianity in answering evaluation questions, although you could use extra reasons from Hinduism.

Topic 3.7.4 Sikhism and family life

As you only need to study one religion, you should only learn one of the four topics on pages 57–60 – the religion you have studied at school.

Key points

The family is important in Sikhism because it was created by God to keep society together, and the family is the main way of keeping Sikhism alive.

Evaluation questions

Evaluation questions will only ask you to refer to one religion, so you would be best just to use Christianity in answering evaluation questions, although you could use extra reasons from Sikhism.

Main points

Family life is important in Sikhism because:

- Sikhism teaches that the family was created by God as the basic unit of society and as the only place in which children should be brought up.
- Sikhs believe that God is present in the home and the Guru Granth Sahib often refers to God as 'our father and mother'.
- The human Gurus married and had families, showing how important the family is.
- The Guru Granth Sahib teaches that family life is the highest form of life.
- Without the family, children would not learn the difference between right and wrong.
- The family is very important for Sikhism to continue and grow as it is the family that brings children into the faith.

Topic 3.8 Christian attitudes to homosexuality

Main points

There are several attitudes to homosexuality in Christianity. The main ones are:

1 The Catholic attitude

The Catholic attitude is that being a homosexual is not a sin but that homosexual sexual activity is a sin. The Catholic Church asks homosexuals to live without any sexual activity and believes they will be helped to do this by the sacraments of the Church. The Church believes that it is sinful to criticise homosexuals or attack their behaviour. Catholics have this attitude because:

- The Bible condemns homosexual sexual activity.
- It is the tradition of the Church that any sexual activity should have the possibility of creating children.
- It is the teaching of the Magisterium which Catholics should believe.
- The Church teaches that people cannot help their sexual orientation, but they can control their sexual activity.
- Discriminating against people because of their sexual orientation is similar to racism, which is sinful.

2 The Evangelical Protestant attitude

Many Evangelical Protestants believe that homosexuality is a sin and that homosexuals can be changed by the power of the Holy Spirit. The reasons for this attitude are:

- The Bible says that homosexuality is a sin and they believe that the Bible is the direct word of God.
- They believe that the salvation of Christ can remove all sins, including homosexuality.
- All the Churches have taught that homosexuality is wrong, even though some now say it is not.

However, the Evangelical Alliance has recently condemned homophobia and said churches should welcome homosexuals.

3 The Liberal Protestant attitude

Many Liberal Protestants welcome homosexuals into the Church, and accept homosexual relationships. Some Liberal Protestants provide blessings for civil partnerships. The reasons for this attitude are:

- They believe that the Bible texts condemning homosexuality show beliefs at the time rather than being the word of God.
- They feel that the major Christian belief in love and acceptance means that homosexuals must be accepted.
- Many believe that if homosexual Christians feel the Holy Spirit approves of their homosexuality, it must be true.
- They believe that Christians should be open and honest and so gay Christians should not be made to tell lies and pretend to be heterosexual.

Key points

- Catholics believe there is nothing wrong with homosexual feelings or relationships as long as there is no sexual activity, because this is the teaching of the Church.
- Evangelical Protestants believe that homosexuality is sinful because it is condemned in the Bible.
- Liberal Protestants believe that homosexuality is acceptable because it is natural, and Christians should love and accept everyone.

61

Evaluation questions

You may be asked to argue for and against giving equal rights to homosexuals (similar arguments could be used for questions on whether Christians or religious people can be homosexual).

1. Arguments for giving equal rights:
   - British law gives equal rights to homosexuals, and equal rights are part of their basic human rights.
   - Medical research has shown that homosexuality is probably genetic and therefore natural, so homosexuals should have equal status and rights.
   - Many liberal Christians feel that the major Christian belief in love and acceptance means that homosexuals must be given equal rights.

2. Arguments against giving equal rights to homosexuals:
   - The Bible condemns homosexual sexual activity, so homosexuals cannot have equal rights.
   - It is the tradition of the Church that any sexual activity should have the possibility of creating children, therefore homosexuals should not be allowed to be sexually active.
   - The Churches have always taught that homosexuality is wrong and so homosexuals should not be given equal rights.

You may also be asked to argue for and against civil partnerships.

1. Arguments for civil partnerships:
   - They allow homosexual couples to commit themselves to each other and encourage stable sexual relationships.
   - They allow homosexual couples to share their belongings, pensions, etc. in just the same way as heterosexual couples.
   - They are a way of encouraging the Christian virtues of love and **faithfulness** among homosexuals.

2. Arguments against civil partnerships:
   - Christianity teaches that God gave marriage for a man and a woman, not two people of the same sex.
   - One of the purposes of Christian marriage is for the procreation of children and as homosexuals cannot procreate, they should not marry.
   - Christians who believe homosexuals should not be sexually active cannot accept civil partnerships because they encourage homosexual sexual activity.

Topic 3.9.1 Islam and homosexuality

Main points

1 The majority attitude
Most Muslims believe that homosexuality is wrong because:

- Homosexuality is condemned by the Qur'an and the Qur'an is the final word of God.
- The Prophet Muhammad condemned homosexuality in several hadith, and Muslims should follow his teachings.
- God says in the Qur'an that marriage between a man and a woman is the only lawful form of sex.
- Islam teaches that any sexual activity should have the possibility of creating children.
- All Muslims should try to have a family, but homosexuals cannot.

2 The minority attitude
Some Muslims believe that homosexuality is acceptable because:

- They believe that Islam is a religion of tolerance, not hate.
- They believe that God created and loves all people whatever their sexual orientation.
- They believe that scientific evidence about homosexuality means that God must have made some people homosexual.

As you only need to study one religion, you should only learn one of the four topics on pages 63–66 – the religion you have studied at school.

Key points

- Most Muslims believe that homosexuality is wrong because it is condemned in the Qur'an and Shari'ah.
- A few Muslims believe that homosexuality should be accepted because it was created by God and Islam is a religion of peace and tolerance.

Evaluation questions

Evaluation questions will only ask you to refer to one religion, so you would be best just to use Christianity in answering evaluation questions, although you could use extra reasons from Islam.

Topic 3.9.2 Judaism and homosexuality

As you only need to study one religion, you should only learn one of the four topics on pages 63–66 – the religion you have studied at school.

Key points

- Orthodox Jews believe that homosexuality is wrong because it is condemned in the Torah and stops people from having families.
- Most Liberal or Reform Jews accept homosexuality because it is natural and Jewish people should respect others.

Evaluation questions

Evaluation questions will only ask you to refer to one religion, so you would be best just to use Christianity in answering evaluation questions, although you could use extra reasons from Judaism.

Main points

There are two different attitudes to homosexuality in Judaism.

1 The Orthodox Jewish view is that being a homosexual is not a sin, but homosexual sexual activity is a sin as is homophobia. They have this attitude because:
   - The Torah condemns homosexual activity and the Torah is the word of God.
   - The Torah and Talmud declare that marriage between a man and a woman is the only lawful form of sex.
   - Judaism teaches that any sexual activity should have the possibility of creating children.
   - It is a mitzvot that Jewish adults should marry and raise a family, which homosexuals cannot do.

2 The Liberal or Reform groups see homosexuality as acceptable because:
   - They believe that the Torah needs to be re-interpreted in the light of modern society.
   - As scientists now believe that sexual orientation is natural, it must be given by God.
   - Jewish people should treat others as they would want to be treated themselves, which must mean accepting homosexuals.
   - They feel that labelling homosexuality as wrong leads to homophobia, which is linked to the evils of racism.

Topic 3.9.3 Hinduism and homosexuality

Main points

There are two attitudes to homosexuality in Hinduism.

1 Most Hindus disapprove of homosexuality and think it should not be practised by Hindus because:
- The Laws of Manu only mention and approve of heterosexual sex.
- All Hindus should pass through the householder stage where one must marry and raise a family – neither of which can a homosexual do.
- Hinduism restricts sexual activity to the householder stage of marriage and family life.
- As homosexuals cannot be householders, they will not be able to attain moksha.

2 Some Hindus believe that homosexuals should be treated the same as heterosexuals because:
- There are sculptures and carvings of homosexual sex (both male and female) in old Hindu temples.
- There are ways to achieve moksha other then being a householder.
- There is a special caste of men called the Hijras who dress and behave as women to serve the mother goddess Parvati.
- As scientists now believe that sexual orientation is natural, it must be given by God.

As you only need to study one religion, you should only learn one of the four topics on pages 63–66 – the religion you have studied at school.

Key points

- Most Hindus believe that homosexuality is wrong because it stops people from fulfilling their duty as householders.
- Some Hindus accept homosexuality because it is natural and could be another way of finding moksha.

Evaluation questions

Evaluation questions will only ask you to refer to one religion, so you would be best just to use Christianity in answering evaluation questions, although you could use extra reasons from Hinduism.

Topic 3.9.4 Sikhism and homosexuality

As you only need to study one religion, you should only learn one of the four topics on pages 63–66 – the religion you have studied at school.

Key points

- Most Sikhs believe that homosexuality is wrong because it stops people from marrying and raising a family.
- Some Sikhs accept homosexuality because it is natural and is not mentioned in the Sikh scriptures.

Evaluation questions

Evaluation questions will only ask you to refer to one religion, so you would be best just to use Christianity in answering evaluation questions, although you could use extra reasons from Sikhism.

Main points

Neither the Guru Granth Sahib, nor the Rahit Maryada say anything about homosexuality, but there are two Sikh attitudes.

1 Many Sikhs still think that homosexuality is wrong because:
   - Sikhism expects all Sikhs to marry and raise a family.
   - The human Gurus married and had families, showing they were heterosexual. Sikhs should follow their examples.
   - Although the Gurus and the Rahit Maryada do not mention homosexuality, they do restrict sex to marriage.

2 Some Sikhs accept homosexuality and think homosexuals should be treated in the same way as anyone else because:
   - If homosexuality is wrong it would have been banned by the Guru Granth Sahib or the Rahit Maryada.
   - They believe that Sikh homosexual rules on marriage and being faithful to one partner should be applied to homosexual partnerships.
   - As scientists now believe that sexual orientation is natural, it must be given by God.
   - Sikhs should respect all of God's creation and so homosexuals should be respected.

Topic 3.10 Christian attitudes to contraception

Main points

There are two main attitudes to contraception among Christians.

1 The Catholic attitude

The Catholic Church has always taught responsible parenthood which involves deciding on how many children to have and when to have them. However, the Catholic way to achieve this is through using natural family planning rather than artificial methods of contraception. Catholics believe this because:

- Pope Pius XI condemned all forms of artificial contraception.
- Pope Pius XII declared that Catholics could use natural methods of contraception.
- Pope Paul VI stated that the only allowable forms of contraception are natural methods, and this teaching has been confirmed in the Catechism of the Catholic Church.
- The Church teaches that all sex should be unitive (bringing the couple together) and creative (bringing new life).
- Some contraceptives bring about a very early abortion (abortifacient).
- The Catholic Church believes artificial contraception leads to sexual **promiscuity**, broken families, divorce and sexually transmitted diseases.

2 The attitude of non-Catholic Christians

Almost all non-Catholic Christians believe that all forms of contraception are permissible because:

- Christianity is about love and justice, and contraception improves women's health and raises the standard of living.
- God created sex for enjoyment and to strengthen marriage so there does not have to be the possibility of creation of children.
- There is nothing in the Bible that forbids the use of contraception.
- In 1930, the Lambeth Conference of the worldwide Anglican Communion (Church of England) said Christians could use contraception to limit family size.
- They believe that using condoms is the best way to combat HIV/AIDS.

Key points

- The Catholic Church teaches that using artificial methods of contraception to stop a baby being conceived is wrong. God gave sex in order to create children.
- Other Christians allow the use of contraception because they believe God gave sex to strengthen a married relationship.

Evaluation questions

For arguments for contraception use the non-Catholic reasons for allowing contraception in the second main point. For arguments against contraception use the Catholic reasons for not allowing contraception in the first main point.

Topic 3.11.1 Islam and contraception

As you only need to study one religion, you should only learn one of the four topics on pages 68–71 – the religion you have studied at school.

Key points

- Some Muslims are against the use of contraceptives because they believe God created sex for procreation.
- Other Muslims agree with contraception because the Prophet and law schools do.

Evaluation questions

Evaluation questions will only ask you to refer to one religion, so you would be best just to use Christianity in answering evaluation questions, although you could use extra reasons from Islam.

Main points

All Muslims believe that they should have children, but there are different attitudes as to whether contraception can be used to limit the number of children.

1   Some Muslims believe that contraception should not be used at all because:
   - They believe the Qur'an's command, 'You should not kill your children for fear of want' means a ban on contraception.
   - They believe that God created sex for having children.
   - They are opposed to abortion and so would not allow any contraceptives that acted as abortifacients.
   - They believe it is the duty of Muslims to have large families.

2   Some Muslims believe that it is permitted for Muslims to use contraception to limit the number of children because:
   - There are several hadith which record that the Prophet permitted the use of coitus interruptus as a means of contraception.
   - The Qur'an says God does not place extra burdens on his followers, and contraception stops extra burdens.
   - If pregnancy risks a mother's health, contraception must be allowed because Islam puts the mother's life first.
   - Muslim lawyers agree that contraception is different from abortion and so should be permitted.

Topic 3.11.2 Judaism and contraception

Main points

There are three different attitudes to contraception in Judaism.

1 Ultra Orthodox Jews do not approve of any form of artificial contraception, unless the mother's health is at risk because:
   - They believe God's command that Jewish people should be fruitful means they should have large families.
   - The Torah says the male sperm is sacred and not to be killed.
   - Many Rabbis teach that God created sex for having children.

2 Orthodox Jews allow women to use contraception after a couple has had two children because:
   - Torah, Talmud and the rabbis teach that the health of the mother should come first.
   - Contraceptives for women do not kill the male seed.
   - It is a mitzvot to have a family and having two children obeys this.

3 Liberal or Reform Jews believe that couples should make their own decisions about contraception because:
   - God expects people to use intelligence and technology to prevent unwanted things from happening.
   - They believe the Torah needs updating and contraception should be available to men and women.
   - It is better to use contraception than to bring unwanted children into the world.

> As you only need to study one religion, you should only learn one of the four topics on pages 68–71 – the religion you have studied at school.

Key points

- Ultra Orthodox Jews do not allow contraception because they believe God wants them to have large families.
- Orthodox Jews only allow female contraception because the Torah says the male seed is sacred.
- Liberal or Reform Jews allow any form of contraception because they believe the Torah should be brought up to date.

Evaluation questions

Evaluation questions will only ask you to refer to one religion, so you would be best just to use Christianity in answering evaluation questions, although you could use extra reasons from Judaism.

Topic 3.11.3 Hinduism and contraception

As you only need to study one religion, you should only learn one of the four topics on pages 68–71 – the religion you have studied at school.

Key points

- Most Hindus allow contraception because contraception does not affect the soul and it helps the population not to exceed the food supply.
- Some Hindus only accept contraceptives which do not kill sperm or eggs because of their beliefs in ahimsa.
- A few Hindus are against all forms of contraception because they believe it is the duty of a householder to have a large family.

Evaluation questions

Evaluation questions will only ask you to refer to one religion, so you would be best just to use Christianity in answering evaluation questions, although you could use extra reasons from Hinduism.

Main points

There are three attitudes to contraception in Hinduism.

1 Most Hindus believe that all forms of contraception are good because they believe:
   - The householder ashrama should be about fulfilling one's dharma, not struggling to cope with a large family.
   - The soul cannot be affected by contraception, as there is no soul before conception.
   - Humans have a duty to make sure that the population does not exceed the food supply.
   - Contraception does not involve violence to a living thing and so it is not against ahimsa.

2 Some Hindus only accept certain forms of contraception, such as the pill and sterilisation, because:
   - They believe that contraceptiives that kill either sperm or eggs are against ahimsa.
   - They are against abortion and so cannot accept abortifacient contraceptives.

3 A few Hindus are against any form of contraception because:
   - They believe that large families are part of the householder ashrama.
   - They believe that sex must involve the possibility of children to fulfil dharma.
   - They believe strongly in ahimsa and think that any contraceptives that kill either sperm or eggs or cause an early abortion are against ahimsa.

Topic 3.11.4 Sikhism and contraception

Main points

There are different attitudes to contraception among Sikhs.

1 Some Sikhs think that it is wrong to use contraceptives because they believe:

- God gave sex to humans to have children.
- Contraception is killing life which is banned in the Guru Granth Sahib.
- Sikhs should follow the example of the human Gurus who had large families.

2 Most Sikhs believe contraceptives can be used to limit family size after two children because:

- They believe life does not begin until the moment of conception.
- The Guru Granth Sahib says that God does not intend humans to suffer and contraception stops suffering.
- Having a small family is still following the examples of the Gurus.

3 Some Sikhs think married Sikhs can use any form of contraception because:

- Contraception is not mentioned in the Guru Granth Sahib or the Rahit Maryada.
- The teaching of the Guru Granth Sahib on God not wanting humans to suffer means that they should only have wanted children.

As you only need to study one religion, you should only learn one of the four topics on pages 68–71 – the religion you have studied at school.

Key points

- Some Sikhs believe contraception is wrong because all sex should allow for the procreation of life.
- Most Sikhs believe that contraceptives can be used to limit family size after two children.
- Some Sikhs believe a married couple can use contraception because it is not mentioned in the Sikh holy book.

Evaluation questions

Evaluation questions will only ask you to refer to one religion, so you would be best just to use Christianity in answering evaluation questions, although you could use extra reasons from Sikhism.

How to answer questions on Section 3

You should already know the basics about how to answer questions from Section 1, pages 15–17, but here is an answer to a whole question on Section 3 with a commentary to help you.

Question a)
What is promiscuity? (2 marks)

Answer
Promiscuity is sleeping around.

> One mark for a partially correct answer.

Answer
Promiscuity is having sex with a number of partners without commitment.

> Two marks for a correct definition.

Question b)
Do you think sex outside marriage is wrong?
Give TWO reasons for your point of view. (4 marks)

Answer
I think sex outside marriage is wrong because adultery is cheating on your marriage partner ...

> One mark for a reason.

... and breaking your wedding vows.

> Two marks because the reason is developed.

Also it is breaking the commandments ...

> Three marks because a second reason is given.

... because the sixth commandment says 'You shall not commit adultery'.

> Four marks because the second reason is developed.

> Total = four marks. Remember! Response questions are really like part (i) of an evaluation question where you only have to give two reasons. To answer a response question, you should just use two reasons from the point of view you agree with in the evaluation questions advice for a topic.

Question c)
Choose one religion other than Christianity and explain why some of its followers agree with divorce and some do not. (8 marks)

Answer
Some Muslims would not divorce because Muhammad is reported to have said that divorce is the most hated of lawful things and they follow what Muhammad said.

> LEVEL 1: two marks for a reason for one attitude expressed in basic English.

Also many Muslims believe they will be sent to hell if they harm their children, and divorce is likely to harm the children.

> LEVEL 2: by giving a second reason for the attitude, the answer goes up to level 2 and because the answer is written in clear English it would gain four marks.

Most Muslims believe that divorce should be allowed because the Qur'an permits divorce and sets out the terms for custody of children and care for divorced wives.

> LEVEL 3: by adding another attitude with a reason the answer moves up to level 3 and, because the answer is written in a clear style of English with some use of specialist vocabulary (Qur'an, Muhammad, lawful things, custody of children), it would gain six marks.

The Shari'ah permits divorce and has many laws about how divorce and re-marriage should operate. Marriage is a contract in Islam and the contract says what is to happen if the couple divorce so divorce must be allowed.

> LEVEL 4: by adding a further reason for the second attitude, the answer moves up to level 4 and, because it is written in a clear and correct style of English with extra specialist vocabulary (Shari'ah, re-marriage, contract), it would gain eight marks – full marks.

Question d)
'Civil partnerships are a good idea.'

(i) Do you agree? Give reasons for your opinion.　　(3 marks)
(ii) Give reasons why some people may disagree with you.　(3 marks)

In your answer, you should refer to at least one religion

Answer

(i) I do agree because a civil partnership allows homosexual couples to commit themselves to each other and encourages stable sexual relationships.

Also civil partnerships allow homosexual couples to share their belongings, pensions, etc. in just the same way as heterosexual couples.

Finally, civil partnerships are a way of encouraging the Christian virtues of love and faithfulness among homosexuals.

(ii) Many Christians would disagree with me because Christianity teaches that God gave marriage for a man and a woman, not two people of the same sex.

One of the purposes of Christian marriage is for the procreation of children and as homosexuals cannot procreate, they cannot marry.

Christians who believe homosexuals should not be sexually active cannot accept civil partnerships because they encourage homosexual sexual activity.

One mark for a personal opinion with a reason.

Another reason is given so it moves up to two marks.

The answer now gives another reason for the opinion, so it moves up to three marks.

One mark for a reason why some people might disagree.

Another reason is given so it moves up to two marks.

The answer now gives another reason for some people disagreeing, so it moves up to three marks.

This answer to question d) can gain full marks because part (i) has one reference to Christianity and part (ii) refers to Christianity.

SECTION 3 TEST

SECTION 3: Marriage and the family

Answer both questions

1. a) What is faithfulness? (2 marks)

   b) Do you think Christians should have sex before marriage? Give two reasons for your point of view. (4 marks)

   c) Explain why some Christians allow divorce and remarriage, but others do not. (8 marks)

   d) 'Religious people should not use contraceptives.'

   (i) Do you agree? Give reasons for your opinion. (3 marks)

   (ii) Give reasons why some people may disagree with you. (3 marks)

   In your answer you should refer to at least one religion.

   (Total: 20 marks)

2. a) What is procreation? (2 marks)

   b) Do you think religious people can be homosexual? Give two reasons for your point of view. (4 marks)

   c) Explain why attitudes to divorce and marriage have changed. (8 marks)

   d) 'Living together is just as good as being married.'

   (i) Do you agree? Give reasons for your opinion. (3 marks)

   (ii) Give reasons why some people may disagree with you. (3 marks)

   In your answer you should refer to at least one religion.

   (Total: 20 marks)

You should now use the mark scheme in Appendix 1, page 98, to mark your answers, and the self-help tables in Appendix 1, pages 99–100, to see how you can improve your performance. If you need more help with the mark scheme for these questions, go to www.hoddereducation.co.uk/religionandlife

Section 4 Religion and community cohesion

KEY WORDS FOR SECTION 4	
Community cohesion	a common vision and shared sense of belonging for all groups in society
Discrimination	treating people less favourably because of their ethnicity/gender/colour/sexuality/age/class
Ethnic minority	a member of an ethnic group (race) which is much smaller than the majority group
Interfaith marriages	marriage where the husband and wife are from different religions
Multi-ethnic society	many different races and cultures living together in one society
Multi-faith society	many different religions living together in one society
Prejudice	believing some people are inferior or superior without even knowing them
Racial harmony	different races/colours living together happily
Racism	the belief that some races are superior to others
Religious freedom	the right to practise your religion and change your religion
Religious pluralism	accepting all religions as having an equal right to coexist
Sexism	discriminating against people because of their gender (being male or female)

Topic 4.1 Changing attitudes to the role of men and women in the United Kingdom

Main points

How attitudes have changed

During the second half of the nineteenth century it became the accepted view that married women should stay at home and look after the children. However, between 1882 and 1975 women have gained the rights to:

- keep their property separate from that of their husband's
- vote in elections and become councillors and MPs
- receive the same pay as men for the same work.

In 1975, the Sex Discrimination Act aimed to reduce **sexism** in society by making it illegal to discriminate in employment on grounds of gender or whether someone is married.

Attitudes to the roles of men and women have been slower to change and women are still more likely to do all the housework, have fewer promotion prospects and lower salaries than men.

Why attitudes have changed

- The work of the suffragette movement showed that women were no longer prepared to be treated as second class citizens.
- During the First and Second World Wars, women had to take on many of the jobs previously done by men and did these jobs just as well as men.
- The development of equal rights for women in other countries made it difficult to claim they were not needed in the UK.
- Social and industrial developments in the 1950s and 1960s led to the need for more women workers.
- The UN Declaration of Human Rights and the development of the feminist movement meant equal rights had to be accepted.
- The Labour governments of 1964–70 and 1974–9 were dedicated to equal rights for women.

Topic 4.2 Christian attitudes to equal rights for women in religion

Main points

There are different attitudes to equal rights for women in religion in Christianity.

1 The traditional attitude of Protestant Christianity

Many Evangelical Protestants teach that men and women have separate and different roles and so cannot have equal rights in religion. Women should not speak in church and only men can be Church leaders and teachers. They have this attitude because:

- In the Bible, St Paul teaches that women should not teach or speak in church.
- St Paul also uses the story of Adam and Eve in Genesis to show that men have been given more rights by God because Adam was created first.
- Although Jesus had women followers, he chose only men as his twelve apostles.
- It has always been the tradition of the Church that only men should be leaders.

2 The modern attitude of Protestant Christianity

Many Protestant Churches (e.g. Church of England, Methodist, United Reformed Church, Baptist) give men and women equal rights, and have women ministers and priests, because:

- The creation story in Genesis 1 says that God created male and female at the same time in his image and therefore of equal status.
- In some of his letters, Paul teaches that men and women are equal in Christ.
- There is evidence from the Gospels that Jesus treated women as his equals, for example:
  - he had women disciples who stayed with him at the cross, unlike the male disciples who ran away
  - after his resurrection, Jesus appeared first to his women disciples.
- There is some evidence that there were women priests in the early Church.

3 Catholic attitudes to the roles of men and women

The Catholic Church teaches that men and women should have equal rights in society and in religion except that they cannot be part of the ordained ministry (deacons, priests and bishops). Catholics have this attitude because:

- The creation story in Genesis 1 says that God created male and female at the same time in his image and therefore of equal status.
- It is the teaching of the Catholic Catechism that men and women are equal, and should have equal rights in life and society.
- Only men can be priests because the apostles were all men, and priests and bishops are successors of the apostles.
- Only men can be priests because Jesus was a man and the priest represents Jesus in the Mass.

Key points

- Traditional Protestants believe only men should be religious leaders because this is what the Bible teaches.
- Liberal Protestants believe men and women should have equal roles in religion because Jesus had women disciples.
- Catholics believe men and women should have equal roles, but only men can become priests because Jesus was a man.

Evaluation questions

For arguments for women having equal rights in religion use the reasons for the modern Protestant attitude and the first two bullets listing the reasons for the Catholic attitude. For arguments against use the reasons for the traditional Protestant attitude and the last two bullets listing the reasons for the Catholic attitude.

Topic 4.3.1 Islam and equal rights for women in religion

As you only need to study one religion, you should only learn one of the four topics on pages 78–81 – the religion you have studied at school.

Main points

There are different attitudes to equal rights for women in religion among Muslims.

1 The traditional attitude

Some Muslims believe that men and women should have different roles in life and religion, and therefore they should have different rights. They believe that women should perform their religious duties (except hajj) in the home and men should worship God in the mosque with their sons and lead the religion. They have this attitude because:

- The Qur'an teaches that men should support women because God has given men a stronger physique.
- The Qur'an teaches that women have been created to bear children and men to provide for them.
- The Qur'an teaches that men need more money than women to be the family providers.
- It is traditional for only men to attend the mosque and to be imams.

2 The modern attitude

Some Muslims believe that men and women should have completely equal rights in religion and education and a few would accept women religious leaders. They have this attitude because:

- The Qur'an teaches that men and women are equal in religion and education.
- There is evidence that Muhammad encouraged both men and women to worship in the mosque.
- There were women religious leaders during the early stages of Islam.
- They have been affected by the non-religious arguments for equal rights for women.

Many British Muslims mix these two attitudes and agree with women having equal rights in everything except religion.

Topic 4.3.2 Judaism and equal rights for women in religion

Main points

There are different attitudes to equal rights for women in religion in Judaism.

1 The Orthodox attitude

Most Orthodox Jews believe that men and women have different roles and so they cannot have equal rights in religion. It is the role of women to keep a kosher home and sit separately from the men in the synagogue. It is the role of men to perform the ritual prayers every day and make sure the synagogue provides all the worship and education needed. Orthodox Jewish women cannot be religious leaders or rabbis. They have this attitude because:

- It is the teaching of the Torah, Talmud and rabbis.
- The mitzvot only apply to men, therefore women cannot have the same rights in religion as men.
- Women cannot form a minyan and so cannot have equal rights with men in the synagogue.
- Women cannot be witnesses in a Bet Din court and so cannot have equal rights with men in the religious laws of Judaism.

2 The Liberal or Reform attitude

In Liberal or Reform and Progressive Judaism, men and women have completely equal rights and there are women rabbis. They have this attitude because:

- The creation story in Genesis 1 says that God created male and female at the same time and of equal status.
- They believe that the Torah needs to be interpreted for today's world, and those parts of the Torah denying equal rights to women should no longer apply.
- They believe that to deny equal rights to women in religion is the same as saying that God prefers men to women.
- They believe that Judaism should relate to attitudes in the modern world and so should accept equal rights for women.

As you only need to study one religion, you should only learn one of the four topics on pages 78–81 – the religion you have studied at school.

Key points

- Orthodox Jews believe that men and women are equal but have different rights in religion because it is the teaching of the Torah.
- Liberal or Reform Jews believe that men and women have completely equal rights in religion and accept women as rabbis because God created men and women with equal status.

Evaluation questions

Evaluation questions will only ask you to refer to one religion, so you would be best just to use Christianity in answering evaluation questions, although you could use extra reasons from Judaism.

Topic 4.3.3 Hinduism and equal rights for women in religion

As you only need to study one religion, you should only learn one of the four topics on pages 78–81 – the religion you have studied at school.

Key points

- Traditional Hindus teach that men and women have different roles in religion because of the Laws of Manu.
- Modern Hindus believe that men and women should have equal roles in religion because all souls are part of the divine and so are equal.

Evaluation questions

Evaluation questions will only ask you to refer to one religion, so you would be best just to use Christianity in answering evaluation questions, although you could use extra reasons from Hinduism.

Main points

There are different attitudes to equal rights for women in religion in Hinduism.

1 The traditional attitude

Some Hindus believe that men and women have different roles and so cannot have equal rights in religion, so they do not allow women to be priests or religious leaders because:

- It is the teaching of the shruti scriptures.
- It is the teaching of the Laws of Manu which must be followed to fulfil your dharma and achieve moksha.
- It is the tradition for the householder ashrama which all Hindus must complete.
- It is part of Indian culture which traditional Hindus regard as part of Hinduism.

2 The modern attitude

Some Hindus (such as Iskcon and the Virashaivas) give women equal rights in both life and religion and have women religious leaders because:

- They believe that all souls are actually or potentially part of the divine and so are equal.
- They believe that even the shruti scriptures need interpreting for today's world.
- They believe that the Laws of Manu were intended for a different time and society.
- They believe there are other ways to gain moksha than following the traditional ashramahs.

Some modern Hindus (such as the Swaminarayan) would say that men and women should have equal rights in other aspects of life, but not in religion.

Topic 4.3.4 Sikhism and equal rights for women in religion

Main points

There are different attitudes to equal rights for women in religion in Sikhism.

1 The religious attitude

Sikhism teaches the complete equality of men and women, and so most Sikhs believe that women should have equal rights in religion because:

- Guru Nanak taught that male and female are to be seen as two halves of a whole who therefore have equal rights.
- Equal rights for women was the teaching of all the other Gurus, e.g. Guru Amar Das appointed women as Sikh preachers and Mati Sahib Kaur mixed the amrit for the first initiation ceremony.
- The Guru Granth Sahib teaches that God is neither male nor female.
- The Guru Granth Sahib teaches that men and women have so much in common that they must be treated the same.

2 The cultural attitude

Some Sikhs believe that men and women should have different roles and so cannot have equal rights in religion. They believe that women should look after the home and children, not be religious leaders because:

- Most Sikhs come from the Punjab where women are not given equal rights to men.
- In Punjabi society, girls are regarded as the property of their father and then their husband.
- It is difficult to change cultural attitudes and some Sikhs believe that culture is part of religion.
- Most Sikhs with this attitude do not read the scriptures, nor know about the lives and teachings of the Gurus.

As you only need to study one religion, you should only learn one of the four topics on pages 78–81 – the religion you have studied at school.

Key points

- Some Sikhs believe that men and women are totally equal and should have the same roles in life and religion because this is the teaching of the Gurus.
- Some Sikhs are affected by cultural attitudes and think women should be subordinate to men and not have a role in religion.

Evaluation questions

Evaluation questions will only ask you to refer to one religion, so you would be best just to use Christianity in answering evaluation questions, although you could use extra reasons from Sikhism.

Topic 4.4 The United Kingdom as a multi-ethnic society

Key points

- Britain has many ethnic minorities and so is a multi-ethnic society.
- Multi-ethnic societies have many benefits, such as advancing more quickly because they have a greater variety of ideas.
- A multi-ethnic society needs equal opportunities and treatment to work, so prejudice and discrimination cause major problems in such a society because they do not treat everyone equally.

Main points

The UK has always been a mixed society: Celts, Romans, Angles, Saxons, Jutes, Danes, Vikings and Normans are all ancestors of the British.

The UK has always believed in human freedom and offered asylum to those suffering persecution. For example, to French Protestants in the seventeenth century and to European Jews escaping Hitler in the 1930s.

In the 2001 Census, only 7.9 per cent of the UK's population came from **ethnic minorities** (although this percentage changes greatly in different areas), and over half of these were born and educated in the UK.

1 The problems of discrimination and racism

- Racially **prejudiced** employers will not give jobs to certain ethnic groups; religiously prejudiced employers will not give jobs to certain religious groups.
- Prejudiced landlords are likely to refuse accommodation to certain ethnic groups or religions.
- If teachers are prejudiced against certain ethnic minorities or religious groups, they will discriminate against them in their teaching, so that those pupils might not achieve the results they should.
- Prejudiced police officers will discriminate against certain ethnic or religious groups, for example by stopping and searching them when they have no real reason for so doing.

The effects of these problems:

- If certain groups feel that they are being treated unfairly by society then they will begin to work against that society.
- Some politicians believe that young black people turn to crime because they feel they will not be able to get good well-paid jobs because of **discrimination**.
- Some politicians believe that young Muslims have been turning to extremist Islamic groups because they feel they have no chance of success in a prejudiced British society.
- **Racism** and discrimination can lead to groups like the BNP (British National Party) stirring up hatred and violence.

If a **multi-ethnic society** is to function well, it must treat all its members fairly and give equal opportunities to all its members.

2 The benefits of living in a multi-ethnic society

Multi-ethnic societies bring far more benefits than problems:

- People of different ethnic groups and nationalities will get to know and like each other, and probably intermarry.
- More progress will be made in a multi-ethnic society because new people will bring in new ideas and new ways of doing things.
- Life is more interesting with a much greater variety of food, music, fashion and entertainment.
- A multi-ethnic society helps people to live and work in a world of multi-national companies and economic interdependence between all nations.

Evaluation questions

You may be asked to argue for and against living in a multi-ethnic society.

1. For arguments for multi-ethnic societies use part 2 above.
2. People who argue against multi-ethnic societies use such arguments as:
   - Different ethnic groups living in one society are likely to come into conflict with each other if they disagree with each other.
   - Each country should be occupied by only one ethnic group so it is their country (however very few countries are occupied by one ethnic group).
   - Multi-ethnic societies can lead to the loss of the culture of the original group (e.g. the effect of non-Cornish ethnic groups living in Cornwall has led to the disappearance of the Cornish language).
   - If every ethnic group had its own country, there would be no conflict.

Topic 4.5 Government action to promote community cohesion in the United Kingdom

Key points

The UK government is promoting community cohesion by:

- passing laws against racism and discrimination
- making community cohesion part of the national curriculum.

Community cohesion is important because without it a multi-ethnic society will become violent and divided.

Main points

A multi-ethnic society needs to promote **community cohesion** in order to remove the problems of prejudice, discrimination and racism. The British government promotes community cohesion by:

- Making community cohesion part of the National Curriculum.
- Appointing cabinet ministers, judges, etc. from ethnic minorities.
- Passing the Race Relations Act which makes it unlawful to discriminate against anyone because of race, colour, nationality, ethnic or national origins; or to stir up racial hatred.
- Passing the Crime and Disorder Act which allows more severe punishment for offences which involve racial or religious hatred.
- Passing the Racial and Religious Hatred Act which makes it an offence to use threatening words or behaviour about religious beliefs or lack of belief.
- Establishing the Equality and Human Rights Commission which works to get rid of discrimination and to build good relations.

Why community cohesion is important for multi-ethnic and multi-faith societies

- Without community cohesion different groups have different ideas about what society should be like and this can lead to violence. For example, in Oldham, Burnley and Bradford this led to racially/religiously motivated street rioting in 2001, which was caused by different groups leading separate lives, ignorance about other communities, weak local leadership and poor policing (Cantle Report).
- The 7 July 2007 London bombers were British citizens who had lost their sense of allegiance to Britain.
- In countries without community cohesion violence becomes a way of life.
- Lack of community cohesion makes it impossible for people to co-operate in the way modern civilised living needs.

Cohesion is therefore about:

- how to avoid the bad effects of prejudice and discrimination
- how to encourage different groups to work together
- how to ensure respect for others while building up loyal citizens of the same society.

Evaluation questions

You may be asked to argue for and against the need for/importance of government action to promote community cohesion.

1. For arguments for the importance of/need for use the reasons listed under 'Why community cohesion is important for multi-ethnic and multi-faith societies'.
2. Those who argue against government action to promote community cohesion are likely to use such arguments as:
   - If people are forced to co-operate, it might lead to fighting and hatred of different groups.

- The UK has always believed in multi-culturalism – allowing people from different ethnic and cultural backgrounds to live in the UK while following their own culture – which avoids conflict.
- It does not matter if different cultural communities follow their own ideas about society as long as they all obey British laws.
- Community cohesion is not possible; the rich have different ideas from the poor, the workers from the employers, etc.

Topic 4.6 Why Christians should help to promote racial harmony

Main points

Christians should try to promote (bring about) racial harmony because:

- In the Parable of the Good Samaritan, Jesus showed that races who hated each other (like the Jews and Samaritans) should love each other as neighbours.
- Jesus treated people of different races equally.
- St Peter had a vision from God, telling him not to discriminate because God has no favourites among the races.
- St Paul taught that all races are equal in Christ since God created all races in his image.
- The Christian Church has members from every race. Over 50 per cent of the world is Christian and 70 per cent of Christians are non-white.
- All the Christian Churches have made statements recently condemning any form of racism or racial discrimination.

Key points

Christians should promote racial harmony because of:

- the teachings of the Bible against racism
- the teachings of the Churches against racism
- the example of Jesus.

Evaluation questions

You are likely to be asked to argue for and against religion/Christianity being the best way to bring about racial harmony.

1. For reasons for the statement use the main points in this topic and the main points from the religion you are studying in Topic 4.7, pages 86–89.
2. Arguments against could include such reasons as:
   - Some Christian groups work against racial harmony, for example the Ku Klux Klan.
- Politics is a better way of bringing about racial harmony, for example the USA now has a black President, but the Catholic Church does not have a black Pope.
- Not everyone is religious and so things like laws which give everyone equal rights are more likely to bring about racial harmony.

Topic 4.7.1 Islam and racial harmony

As you only need to study one religion, you should only learn one of the four topics on pages 86–89 – the religion you have studied at school.

Key points

Muslims should promote racial harmony because Islam teaches that racism is wrong because of the teachings of the Qur'an and the example of Muhammad.

Evaluation questions

Evaluation questions will only ask you to refer to one religion, so you would be best just to use Christianity in answering evaluation questions, although you could use extra reasons from Islam.

Main points

There are many reasons why Muslims should try to promote racial harmony:

- The Qur'an teaches that God created the whole of humanity from one pair of humans, therefore all races are related and none can be regarded as superior.
- In his final sermon, Muhammad said that every Muslim is a brother to every other Muslim, and so there should be no racism among Muslims.
- Islam teaches that all Muslims form one brotherhood, the Ummah. This means that all Muslims, whatever their race, should regard each other as brothers and sisters.
- Islam is against any form of racism and Muslim leaders and local mosques work with various groups to promote racial harmony in the UK.

Topic 4.7.2 Judaism and racial harmony

Main points

Although most followers of Judaism are also members of the Jewish race (although not necessarily the same ethnic group), Judaism promotes racial harmony because:

- The Torah teaches racial harmony. It shows that all humans can be traced back to Adam and Eve and so they must all be brothers and sisters.
- Most rabbis teach that as God is one, so humanity is one because it was created by the one God.
- There is a lot of teaching in the Tenakh about how God cares for the oppressed and wants his people to bring justice to the world.
- The Jewish people have been given a special responsibility by God to show God's laws to the rest of humanity and part of this responsibility must be promoting racial harmony.

As you only need to study one religion, you should only learn one of the four topics on pages 86–89 – the religion you have studied at school.

Key points

Jewish people should promote racial harmony because Judaism teaches that racism is wrong because of the teachings of the Torah and Jewish experiences in the Holocaust.

Evaluation questions

Evaluation questions will only ask you to refer to one religion, so you would be best just to use Christianity in answering evaluation questions, although you could use extra reasons from Judaism.

Topic 4.7.3 Hinduism and racial harmony

As you only need to study one religion, you should only learn one of the four topics on pages 86–89 – the religion you have studied at school.

Key points

Hindus should promote racial harmony because they believe that every soul is a part of Brahman and so everyone should be treated equally.

Evaluation questions

Evaluation questions will only ask you to refer to one religion, so you would be best just to use Christianity in answering evaluation questions, although you could use extra reasons from Hinduism.

Main points

There are many reasons why Hindus should try to promote racial harmony:

- Hindus believe that every soul is an actual or potential part of the divine (Brahman), so every soul must be of equal value, whatever the person's race or colour.
- The Indian Hindus suffered from racist treatment when they were ruled by the Moghul Empire and then the British Empire, and this treatment has led Hindu leaders to work for racial harmony.
- Although the majority of Hindus are from India, there are many different ethnic groups in India. Gandhi, who led the struggle for Indian independence, taught that the different racial and ethnic groups in India must work and live together as equals.
- Hinduism is opposed to racism and racial discrimination in any form. Hindus work with many other groups in the UK to promote racial harmony.

Topic 4.7.4 Sikhism and racial harmony

Main points

Although most followers of Sikhism are also ethnic Punjabis, Sikhism is opposed to racism and racial discrimination in any form. Sikhs work to promote racial harmony because:

- The Gurus all opposed the caste system and treated all groups as equals.
- Guru Nanak emphasised that anyone from any race can come to salvation.
- In every Sikh act of worship everyone, whatever their race, eats from the same bowl, and sits together in the langar.
- The Guru Granth Sahib teaches that different religions and races should live in harmony.
- Sikhism teaches that because there is only one God who created the whole of humanity, humanity must also be one.

As you only need to study one religion, you should only learn one of the four topics on pages 86–89 – the religion you have studied at school.

Key points

Sikhs should promote racial harmony because Sikhism teaches that racism is wrong because of the teachings of the Guru Granth Sahib and the teachings and examples of the ten human Gurus.

Evaluation questions

Evaluation questions will only ask you to refer to one religion, so you would be best just to use Christianity in answering evaluation questions, although you could use extra reasons from Sikhism.

Topic 4.8 The United Kingdom as a multi-faith society

Main points

Many societies were mono-faith (having only one religion) until the twentieth century, but Britain has had believers in different faiths for many years and by the end of the twentieth century Muslims, Jews, Hindus, Sikhs, Buddhists and other religions were settled in the UK, so that it is a truly **multi-faith society**.

The benefits of living in a multi-faith society

- People can learn about other religions and this can help them to see what religions have in common.
- People from different religions may practise their religion more seriously and this may make people think about how they practise their own religion.
- People may come to understand why different religions believe what they do and this may make people think more seriously about their own beliefs.
- People are likely to become a lot more understanding about and respectful of each other's religions.
- **Religious freedom** and understanding will exist in a multi-faith society and this may help to stop religious conflicts.
- A multi-faith society may even make some people think more about religion as they come across religious ideas they have never thought about before.

Evaluation questions

You are likely to be asked to argue for and against living in a multi-faith society.

1. To argue for living in a multi-faith society, use the reasons listed under 'The benefits of living in a multi-faith society'.

2. People who are firm believers in one religion might be against multi-faith societies because:
   - They encourage your children to look at other religions, and your children might desert your religion.
   - Children from different religions may want to marry each other, and interfaith marriages can create problems for religious parents.
   - They can make it difficult to follow your religion because society cannot be organised for every religion's different rules.
   - They can make it difficult for you to spread your faith because people from other religions might object to you saying that your religion is the best one.

Topic 4.9 Issues raised for religion by a multi-faith society

Main points

For a multi-faith society to work, people need to have the same rights regardless of the religion they do or do not belong to (**religious pluralism**). A multi-faith society cannot accept any one religion as being the true one, and the people living in the society must be free to choose or reject any or all of the religions practised in the society. This can raise a number of issues for religion.

Conversion

1   Many religions see it as their duty, to convert everyone because:
   - They believe that their religion is the only true religion.
   - They believe that the only way for the followers of other religions to get to heaven is for them to be converted.
   - Their holy books teach them that they should convert non-believers.

2   Trying to convert other religions can cause major problems because:
   - Treating people differently because of their religion and trying to convert other religions is discriminating against those who do not have the same faith as you.
   - It is impossible to say all other religions are wrong unless you have studied all of them and no one who is trying to convert others has done this.
   - Trying to convert others can lead to arguments and even violence when people are told their religion is wrong.

Bringing up children

A multi-faith society requires everyone (including children) to have religious freedom and be able to choose which religion to follow, or to reject religion. It also requires that children should learn about the different religions in the society. This causes problems for many religious believers because:

- Most religions encourage parents to ensure that their children are brought up in their religion, and become members of it.
- Most religions teach that only those who follow their religion will have a good life after death, and parents worry what will happen to their children after death if they do not stay in their religion.
- Social and peer pressure compel parents to exert pressure on their children to remain in the faith.
- Children educated in state schools are tempted away from religious lifestyles into the lifestyles of other non-religious teenagers.

> ## Key points
>
> A multi-faith society needs to have laws giving equal rights to all religions and to those who have no religion (religious pluralism). However, a multi-faith society can raise problems for religious people in areas such as:
>
> - conversion attempts by other faiths because it is like discrimination
> - bringing up children because they may leave their parents' faith
> - interfaith marriages because of having to decide which faith the children should be brought up in.

Interfaith marriages

In a multi-faith society, young people of different faiths are going to meet, fall in love and want to marry. This can raise problems because:

- Often both couples must be members of the same religion to have a religious wedding ceremony.
- There is a question of which religion the children of the marriage will be brought up in.
- There is also the problem of what will happen to the couple after death.
- The parents and relatives of the couple often feel that they have been betrayed.

Unless these issues are dealt with, then religion itself can be working against community cohesion and promoting conflict and hatred.

Evaluation questions

You may be asked to argue for and against having the right to convert others.

1. For arguments for having the right, use the reasons listed in point 1 under 'Conversion'.

2. For arguments against, use the reasons listed in point 2 under 'Conversion'.

You may be asked to argue for and against having the right to bring up children in one faith only.

1. For arguments in favour of the right, use the reasons listed under 'Bringing up children'.

2. The main arguments against, children being brought up in one faith only include:
   - It is a human right to have freedom of religion and so children need to learn about more than one religion before they choose which to follow, or not follow.
   - A multi-faith society needs its members to respect all religions and children need to learn about other religions if they are to respect the followers of that religion.

- Children who are brought up knowing only one religion cannot really believe it because they have not compared it with anything else, so they cannot know that it is the best religion.

You may be asked to argue for and against interfaith marriages.

1. The main arguments for interfaith marriages are:
   - It is a human right to be able to marry anyone you want to (especially if you are in love with them).
   - Interfaith marriages will encourage community cohesion as families from different faiths become one family.
   - The children of interfaith marriages will have true religious freedom as they learn about both their parents' religions and can choose between them.

2. For arguments against the statement use the reasons listed under 'Interfaith marriages'.

Topic 4.10 Ways in which religions work together to promote community cohesion in the United Kingdom

Main points

The different religions in the UK are beginning to work to promote community cohesion in the following ways.

1   Different religions are beginning to work with other religions to try to discover what is the same in their religions (e.g. Judaism, Islam and Christianity believe in the prophets Abraham and Moses), and from this work out ways of living together without trying to convert each other. For example, when Pope Benedict XVI addressed a meeting of envoys from the Muslim world in October 2007, he expressed his respect for Muslims and said that the future of the world depends on Christians and Muslims talking and working together.

2   Some religious groups are developing ways of helping interfaith marriages.
   - Many Protestant Churches and Liberal or Reform Jewish synagogues have special wedding services for mixed faith couples.
   - The Church of England now has 'Guidelines for the celebration of interfaith marriages in church'.
   - The website www.interfaithmarriage.org.uk offers help and advice to couples from different religions.

3   The problem of bringing up children is being dealt with in different ways.
   - Some Protestant Christian Churches and Liberal or Reform Jewish synagogues encourage mixed faith parents to bring up their children in both faiths.
   - Leaders from the Church of England, Hindu, Sikh, Catholic, Muslim, Jewish and Buddhist faiths have agreed to follow the National Framework on Religious Education so that children in faith schools will now be taught the main religions practised in the UK.

4   The main way in which religions are trying to promote community cohesion is through working together in special groups.
   - National groups, such as the Inter Faith Network for the UK which was founded in 1987, promote good relations between people of different faiths in this country.
   - Most towns and cities have groups that bring together different faiths in an area, for example the Glasgow Forum of Faiths.
   - There are individual places of worship which work together.

Key points

Religions are working for community cohesion in the UK by:
- working to discover what is the same about religions
- helping with interfaith marriages
- making sure that all children learn about different faiths
- joining local and national groups to promote community cohesion.

Evaluation questions

You may be asked to argue for and against whether religions are doing enough to promote community cohesion in the UK.

1. You can use any of the points above to argue that they are doing enough to promote community cohesion.

2. The main arguments against are:
   - All religions have groups that are still teaching that all other religions are wrong.
   - Most people in Christianity, Islam, etc. are unaware of what is going on with other faiths; it is only a few leaders who are involved in the work.
   - Few religious believers look at the beliefs of other religions and try to work out which is true.
   - Most religious groups are too busy looking after their own followers to try to make links with other faiths.

93

Topic 4.11 How an issue from religion and community cohesion has been dealt with in the media

Key points

When studying the presentation of an issue from religion and community cohesions in the media, you must be able to explain:

- why the issue was chosen
- how it was presented
- whether the presentation treated religious beliefs fairly
- whether the presentation treated religious people fairly.

Main points

You have to study how *one* issue from religion and community cohesion has been presented in *one* form of the media.

From your class notes you should have:

- Notes on why the issue is important and why you think the producers decided to focus on this issue.
- An outline of how the issue was presented, listing the main events and the way the events explored the issue.
- Notes on the way religious beliefs are treated in the presentation of the issue.
- Four pieces of evidence on whether you think the presentation was fair to religious beliefs.
- Four pieces of evidence on whether you think the presentation was fair to religious people.

Evaluation questions

Although you are unlikely to be asked an evaluation question on this topic, if you were, it would be about whether the media treats religious beliefs or people fairly.

1. To argue for fair treatment you should use:
   - The evidence you have from your form of the media for the religious beliefs being treated fairly.
   - The evidence you have from your form of the media for religious people being treated fairly.

2. To argue against fair treatment you should use:
   - The evidence you have from your form of the media for the religious beliefs not being treated fairly.
   - The evidence you have from your form of the media for religious people not being treated fairly.

How to answer questions on Section 4

You should already know the basics about how to answer questions from Section 1, pages 15–17, but here is an answer to a whole question on Section 4 with a commentary to help you.

Question a)
What is community cohesion? (2 marks)

Community cohesion is everybody working together.

> One mark for a partially correct answer.

Community cohesion is a common vision and shared sense of belonging for all groups in society.

> Two marks for a correct definition.

Question b)
Do you think people should be able to marry someone from a different religion? Give TWO reasons for your point of view. (4 marks)

People should be able to marry someone from a different religion because it is a human right ...

> One mark for a reason.

... to be able to marry someone you are in love with.

> Two marks because the reason is developed.

Also interfaith marriages will encourage community cohesion ...

> Three marks because a second reason is given.

... as families from different faiths become one family.

> Four marks because the second reason is developed.

> Total = four marks. Remember! Response questions are really like part (i) of an evaluation question where you only have to give two reasons. To answer a response question, you should just use two reasons from the point of view you agree with in the evaluation questions advice for a topic.

Question c)
Choose one religion other than Christianity and explain why some of its followers agree with equal rights for women in religion and some do not. (8 marks)

Some Muslims believe that men and women should have different rights in life and religion because the Qur'an teaches that men should support women because God has given men a stronger physique.

> LEVEL 1: two marks for a reason for one attitude expressed in basic English.

The Qur'an also teaches that women have been created to bear children, and men to provide for them. This is why it is traditional for only men to attend the mosque and to be imams.

> LEVEL 2: by giving a second reason for the attitude, the answer goes up to level 2 and because the answer is written in clear English it would gain four marks.

Some Muslims believe that men and women should have completely equal rights in religion because the Qur'an teaches that men and women are equal in religion and education.

> LEVEL 3: by adding another attitude with a reason the answer moves up to level 3 and because the answer is written in a clear style of English with some use of specialist vocabulary (Qur'an, mosque, imam) it would gain six marks.

Also there is evidence that Muhammad encouraged both men and women to worship in the mosque, and that there were women religious leaders during the early stages of Islam.

> LEVEL 4: by adding a further reason for the second attitude, the answer moves up to level 4 and because it is written in a clear and correct style of English with more specialist vocabulary (Muhammad, mosque, religious leaders) it would gain eight marks – full marks.

Question d)

'All societies should be multi-faith societies.'

(i) Do you agree? Give reasons for your opinion.   (3 marks)
(ii) Give reasons why some people may disagree with you.   (3 marks)

In your answer, you should refer to at least one religion.

Answer

(i) *I do agree because people from different religions may practise their religion more seriously and this may make people think about how they practise their own religion.*

Also people may come to understand why different religions believe what they do and this may make people think more seriously about their own beliefs.

Finally, people are likely to become a lot more understanding about and respectful of each other's religions.

(ii) *Some Christians might disagree with me because they promised at baptism to bring their children up as Christians and a multi-faith society might encourage their children to look at other religions, and desert Christianity.*

They might also worry that their children might want to marry someone from a different religion, and interfaith marriages can cause lots of problems for religious parents.

They might also worry that a multi-faith society would make it difficult to follow Christianity because society cannot be geared up to just one religion.

One mark for a personal opinion with a reason.

Another reason is given so it moves up to two marks.

The answer now gives another reason for the opinion, so it moves up to three marks.

One mark for a reason why some people might disagree.

Another reason is given so it moves up to two marks.

The answer now gives another reason for some people disagreeing, so it moves up to three marks.

This answer to question d) can gain full marks because part (ii) refers to Christianity.

SECTION 4 TEST

SECTION 4: Religion and community cohesion

Answer both questions

1. a) What is an ethnic minority? (2 marks)

   b) Do you think men and women should have equal roles in life?
   Give two reasons for your point of view. (4 marks)

   c) Explain why racism and discrimination bring problems to a multi-ethnic society. (8 marks)

   d) 'It is easy for different religions to work together in the UK.'
   (i) Do you agree? Give reasons for your opinion. (3 marks)
   (ii) Give reasons why some people may disagree with you. (3 marks)
   In your answer you should refer to at least one religion.

   (Total: 20 marks)

2. a) What is interfaith marriage? (2 marks)

   b) Do you think Christians should work for racial harmony?
   Give two reasons for your point of view. (4 marks)

   c) Explain how the government is working to promote community cohesion in the UK. (8 marks)

   d) 'If everyone were religious, there would be no racism.'
   (i) Do you agree? Give reasons for your opinion. (3 marks)
   (ii) Give reasons why some people may disagree with you. (3 marks)
   In your answer you should refer to at least one religion.

   (Total: 20 marks)

You should now use the mark scheme in Appendix 1, page 98, to mark your answers, and the self-help tables in Appendix 1, pages 99–100, to see how you can improve your performance. If you need more help with the mark scheme for these questions, go to www.hoddereducation.co.uk/religionandlife

Appendix 1

Mark scheme for section tests

a) questions (2 marks)

Use the key words list on page 2 for Section 1, page 19 for Section 2, page 43 for Section 3, page 75 for Section 4.
Award 2 marks for a correct answer.

b) questions (4 marks)

- A personal response with one brief reason award 1 mark.
- A personal response with two brief reasons award 2 marks.
- A personal response with one developed reason award 2 marks.
- For a personal response with two reasons with one developed award 3 marks.
- For a personal response with two developed reasons award 4 marks.

c) questions (8 marks)

- Level 1: for a brief reason in basic English award 2 marks.
- Level 2: for two brief reasons in basic English award 4 marks.
- Level 3: for three brief reasons written in a clear style with some specialist vocabulary award 5 or 6 marks depending on the Quality of Written Communication (QWC).
- Level 4: for four brief reasons written in a clear and correct style of English with a correct use of specialist vocabulary award 7 or 8 marks depending on the QWC.

d) questions (6 marks)

Part (i)
- One reason award 1 mark.
- Two reasons award 2 marks.
- Three reasons award 3 marks.

Part (ii)
- One reason award 1 mark.
- Two reasons award 2 marks.
- Three reasons award 3 marks.

How to improve your performance

When you have completed each test, make a copy of this table and fill it in using your marks.

	Question 1	Question 2
1. How many marks did I get for question a)?		
2. How many marks did I get for question b)? If less than 4:		
• Did I forget to give reasons?		
• Did I forget to develop my reasons?		
3. How many marks did I get for question c)? If less than 8:		
• Did I forget to use specialist vocabulary?		
• Did I describe instead of explain?		
• Did I misunderstand the question?		
• Did I give too few reasons?		
• Did I forget about the Quality of Written Communication?		
4. How many marks did I get for question d)? If less than 6:		
• Did I forget to make one point of view be from one religion?		
• Did I forget to use information from the book?		
• Did I give too few reasons for part (i)?		
• Did I give too few reasons for part (ii)?		

Now use your completed table to complete a copy of this sheet which will show you what you need to do to improve:

HOW TO IMPROVE MY PERFORMANCE

Using the mark table, circle the targets that apply to you.

1. Question a)

Marks	Target
4 or more marks	Make sure I still know all the key words
3 or fewer marks	Learn the key words more thoroughly

2. Question b)

Marks	Target
Yes to bullet point 1	Remember to give reasons for my opinion
Yes to bullet point 2	Make sure I write developed reasons for my opinion

3. Question c)

Marks	Target
Yes to bullet point 1	Remember to use the key words in my part c) answers Learn and use specialist terms
Yes to bullet point 2	Practise understanding questions so that I explain why or how
Yes to bullet point 3	Make sure you read the question carefully and answer what it asks for, not what you want it to ask for
Yes to bullet point 4	Make sure to give four reasons
Yes to bullet point 5	Remember to take care with spelling and punctuation Remember not to use bullet points

4. Question d)

Marks	Target
Yes to bullet point 1	Make sure that either your own point of view or the one which disagrees with you is from a named religion
Yes to bullet point 2	Make sure to use reasons from the revision guide
Yes to bullet point 3 or 4	Make sure to give three reasons for each part